Living Lessons

Edited By Lynn C. Johnston

A Whispering Angel Book

Living Lessons

Copyright © 2010 by Whispering Angel Books as an anthology.

Rights to the individual stories and poems reside with the authors themselves. This collection contains works submitted to the Publisher by individual authors who confirm that the work is their original creation. Based on the authors' confirmations and the Publisher's knowledge, these pieces were written as credited. Whispering Angel Books does not guarantee or assume any responsibility for verifying the authorship of any work.

Views expressed in each work are solely that of the contributor. The publisher does not endorse any political viewpoint or religious belief over another.

All rights reserved under International and Pan-American copyright conventions. No part of this book may be used or reproduced by any means, graphic, electronic, or mechanical including photocopying, recording, taping or by any storage retrieval system without written permission of the publisher except in the case of brief quotations embodied in critical reviews and articles.

ISBN: 978-0-9841421-5-6 (Print)
ISBN: 978-0-9841421-2-5 (Ebook)

Whispering Angel Books
2416 W. Victory Blvd #234
Burbank, CA 91506
http://www.whisperingangelbooks.com

Printed in the United States of America

Whispering Angel Books is dedicated to publishing uplifting and inspirational works for its readers while donating a portion of its book sales to charitable organizations promoting physical, emotional and spiritual healing. If you'd like to learn more about our books or our fundraising programs for your charity, please visit our website: www.whisperingangelbooks.com

*"What you leave behind is not what is
engraved in stone monuments,
but what is woven into the lives of others."*

~ Pericles

TABLE OF CONTENTS

DEDICATION iii

ACKNOWLEDGMENTS iv

INTRODUCTION
    Lynn C. Johnston vii

CROSS ROADS
    Madeleine Kuderick 1

PEACE FOR JIMMY
    Paula Timpson 3

THE REUNION
    Carolyn T. Johnson 4

FOR MATTIE J. T. STEPANEK
    Justin Blackburn 7

MARC'S GRANDFATHER
    Rosalie Ferrer Kramer 8

LIE IN FEAR
    Elsie Valentine 9

THE BLESSINGS OF A DEAR HEART
    Jeanine L. DeHoney 11

BEND
    Lisa Miles 13

AN ANGEL UNAWARE
    Diana M. Amadeo 14

LIFE IS WHAT IT IS
    Belinda Sue 16

LASTING LESSONS FROM A LITTLE SISTER
    Ysabel de la Rosa 17

TRULY BLESSED
    Lynn C. Johnston 20

WINSTON
Judy Kirk 21

THE GREENHORN
Florence Reiss Kraut..22

ROLE MODEL
Mary Elizabeth Laufer..25

BUBBA'S LESSONS
Beckie A. Miller...26

SELF PORTRAIT
Robin Brown...29

TWO LEFT SHOES
E. Baker 31

MY PROVERBS 31 GRANDMOTHER
Francine L. Billingslea...34

ONE MORE STEP
Glenda Barrett..37

RECYCLING
A. Frank Bower 40

LETTER TO MY FIFTH GRADE TEACHER
Michael S. Glaser..43

IN THE MATTER OF LOVE AND REGRET
Andrea L. Watson 45

A SOFT PLACE TO LAND
Abi L. Rexrode...48

BRICK
Bridges DelPonte...51

MATRON SAINT OF THE THROW AWAY
Claudia B. Van Gerven 54

INSPIRATION
    Cynthia Hollamon-Cook..55

A TASTE OF UNCONDITIONAL LOVE
    Elaine Morgan...57

WITCH OR ANGEL
    Eric G. Müller..59

A VOICE FROM THE PAST
    Elayne Clift...62

WHEREVER YOU GO, THERE YOU ARE
    Janet Tamez..64

LIFE LESSON:
  LIGHTING THE INTERNAL SPARK OF HOPE
    Karen R. Elvin..67

MATRIARCH
    Bob Moreland...69

WHEN SILENCE SPEAKS
    Kathleen Gerard..71

VAYA CON DIOS
    Terri Elders...74

NIGHT AND DAY
    Susan Mahan..77

DAD
    Paula Timpson..78

PINK COCONUT SNO-BALLS
    Kellye Blankenship...79

MODELING THE POSSIBLE:
  AN INTERGENERATIONAL INSPIRATION
    Judy Shepps Battle...82

STILL AROUND
    Marsha Pearl Jamil 84

HE CAME HOME
    Jan Cline 85

PERHAPS FORGIVENESS SUSTAINS
    Liz Rose Dolan 87

HONING THE HULA
    Meredith Escudier 88

DUTY
    Skip Hughes 90

OY, THE RUST IN THE GOLDEN YEARS
    Constance Gilbert 93

A PASSIONATE TEACHER
    Barbara Mayer 96

TRIVIAL PURSUITS
    Ben Humphrey 98

OBEDIENCE AND WILLINGNESS
    Naty Matos 99

BEFORE SHE SAID GOODBYE
    Jessica Katsonga Phiri 101

COLLEGE DAYS
    Dale S. Johnson 103

SURVIVAL
    Robert D. Fertig 105

MARTIN LUTHER KING JR
    Justin Blackburn 107

MY OWN RACE
    Rebekah Crain 108

THE HAT
    Elynne Chaplik-Aleskow 110

PERSPECTIVE
    Louise Borad Gerber 113

GRANDPA'S WORDS AND ACTIONS
    William Ricci 114

TRINKETS
    Lottie Corley 117

MARTI'S JEWELS
    Charlotte Jones 118

TO A LOVED ONE
    Sharon Bourke 120

MISS "H."
    Cherise Wyneken 121

DR. CHARLES LYNCH: A MEMOIR
    Dr. Milton Burnett 122

THE PAINT BOX
    Helen R. Carson 125

HE'S STILL HERE
    Dana Taylor 127

NEVER GIVE UP
    Lorraine Quirke 128

HE CALLED ME PRINCESS
    Susan Mahan 131

FOR ELENA MY SISTER IN ITZAPA, GUATEMALA
    Carolyn Ingram 133

WRESTLING WITH AN ANGEL
    Neil Whitman 134

RANDOM ACTS OF KINDNESS
    Carolyn T. Johnson 136

ANAFGHAT'S STORY
    Ann Reisfeld Boutté 139

THE DAY MY UNCLE HANK SAT DOWN TO LUNCH
    WITH HELEN KELLER INA CAFÉ IN THE PHILIPPINES,
    AUGUST 1948
    Paul Hostovsky 141

THE ART OF BEING A GRANDMOTHER
    Joanne Seltzer 143

GRANDMA ESTHER
    Laurie Lee Didesch 144

THE LITTLEST AMBASSADOR
    Lucille Joyner 145

THE TOUGH PART OF EASY
    Lucy Jubilee Barnett 147

EXPOSE YOUR FOIBLES
    Melanie Rigney 149

POETRY IN MOTION
    Eve Hall 150

BECOMING NOBODY
    Rebekah Crain 153

LOVE LEARNED
    Tina Traster 155

REACHING FOR THE STARS
    Tom Leskiw 159

WHEN WE LOVE
    Kimberly Alfrey 162

PILLARS HOLD UP A HOUSE
Leslie Golding Mastroianni 164

DOGS BARK; THE CARAVAN PASSES
Erika Hoffman 167

ABOUT THE CONTRIBUTORS. 171

WE WANT TO HEAR FROM YOU 188

DEDICATION

This book is dedicated to the people who taught us endurance, courage, strength, hope and love through their words and actions – and to those who wish to preserve those "living lessons" by continuing their legacy.

ACKNOWLEDGMENTS

The creation and development of this book would not have been possible without the assistance of many people. I would like to thank everyone who submitted their heartfelt stories and poems for this anthology. With hundreds of wonderful pieces to choose from, each prospective contributor made the selection process far more challenging and rewarding than imaginable.

My deepest appreciation goes out to Julie G. Beers and Ed Johnston for sharing their expertise, opinions and support during this process.

INTRODUCTION

We are dependent on others all our lives. As infants, we rely on them for our physical survival. As we grow, they teach us everything from reading and writing to developing compassion and coping with grief. They shape our values, our character, our beliefs, our perceptions of the world – and even our feelings about our own self worth.

Some of life's most important lessons are taught to us indirectly by those closest to us. We absorb the cumulative influence of our parents, grandparents and siblings as they go about their daily lives leading us by their examples. We are also influenced by our friends, teachers, neighbors and even our own children. And some of life's most profound lessons can come from those we least expect – our acquaintances. They enter our lives for a brief moment but end up changing us forever.

Whether these life lessons make us smile, cry, think or laugh, they endure in our hearts and minds for the rest of our lives, influencing generations to come.

For me, one of my greatest lessons was instilled by my high school drama teacher. Mr. Stewart did more than just teach acting technique, he taught me the importance of challenging myself and he introduced me to the concept of "pushing the envelope."

One day while I was outside of his office socializing with my friends, a student approached Mr. Stewart about changing the acting scene he had been assigned for class. He pleaded his case, but to no avail; Mr. Stewart held his ground, and the student left his office dejected.

The student's desire to change his assignment was not an uncommon one. My friends and I understood his feelings and lamented his situation. Sometimes it seemed like Mr. Stewart deliberately gave us scenes from plays we'd never heard of, paired us with partners we didn't like, and assigned us to portray strange characters we didn't understand.

Overhearing us discuss this student's plight, Mr. Stewart approached us to explain. "Do you want to know why I wouldn't change his scene?"

We were all eager to hear his response. "Because I knew it would be a challenge for him."

We stood there unimpressed. "He hated his assignment because he was presented with a new situation, and he doesn't know how to deal with it yet," he said.

Our teenage faces stared back blankly. "When people are given a new challenge, they usually try to get out of it," Mr. Stewart continued. "When they realize that isn't going to work and they are forced to confront their situation, they resent it." That was a feeling we could all understand.

"Once they start figuring out how to overcome their challenge, they don't hate it anymore; in fact, it becomes enjoyable." Then he paused briefly. "And once they've overcome it, they feel good about their accomplishment."

I don't think I really absorbed the full impact of his explanation at the time, but it did begin to spark a greater awareness of my own reactions to change and challenge.

Even today, decades later, I have to pause whenever I am confronted with a new situation that I instantly "hate." I hear his words echo in mind. Then I ask myself if I really "hate" the situation or am I just upset about being challenged with a situation that I don't know how address yet.

More often than not, it is the latter. Then I take a deep breath, send out a silent thank you to Mr. Stewart and begin "pushing the envelope." It's in those moments that I can recognize and truly appreciate my life lessons.

The poems and stories in Living Lessons serve as a powerful testament to the enduring legacy of the people who have touched our lives. Whether their influence took a minute or a lifetime, they taught us about tenacity, encouragement, bravery, compassion, love and so much more, permanently changing our hearts and minds with their precious living lessons. And, for that, we will be forever grateful.

- Lynn C. Johnston

CROSS ROADS
By Madeleine Kuderick

My family had just moved to Oak Park and as a shy seven-year-old, I dreaded being the *new kid* at Hatch Elementary School. My stomach twisted in knots as I trudged down the block, past the big, blue mailbox, and over to the busy intersection at Ridgeland Avenue. The brick school building loomed across the street and, I could hear the shouts of gigantic sixth graders on the playground, probably waiting to trample me. I wanted to turn around and run back home. But then, I saw Frosty.

I'd never seen a crossing guard before. Not up close anyway. But there she was, walking across the street, bending down to shake my hand. When she leaned in, I could see the blue sparkle of her eyes and smell the powdery scent of skin cream on her cheeks.

"Everybody calls me Frosty," she said. Then, she gave my hand a little squeeze. "You'll do just great today!"

I don't know why, but somehow I believed her.

A smile spread across Frosty's face and the wrinkles around her eyes deepened. She pulled a peppermint from her pocket and slipped it in my hand.

"I'll have another piece of candy waiting for you after school," she promised. "Then, you can tell me all about your day."

I stood on the corner as Frosty marched back to the middle of the busy intersection and stretched her arms out wide. She looked strong and important wearing her dark blue uniform with silver buttons and bright, white gloves. The cars slowed to a stop and Frosty ushered me safely across the street.

I don't remember anything else about my first day at Hatch Elementary School. But, I do remember meeting Frosty.

As time went on, I began to look forward to those comings and goings across Ridgeland Avenue. Don't get me wrong. I never really got over being the new kid at school and spent most of my elementary years as the last student picked for Phys Ed teams and the first one to be teased. Still, I always felt a rush of excitement when the school bell rang. I'd run to the mulberry tree at the end of the playground and wait until the other kids crossed the street. Then, when I had Frosty all to myself, I'd tell her how I got an A minus on my spelling test or that I won a goldfish at the church carnival. Sometimes, I'd slip a poem in her pocket, something I'd written just for her. Frosty would pat the paper inside her uniform and tell me how she'd treasure my words.

"I know you're going to be a writer one day," Frosty assured me.
And somehow, I believed her.

Over time, I came to rely on those moments and the comfort of our routine. Peppermints on Mondays. Butterscotch on Wednesdays. A stick of gum on Fridays when I walked an extra block to my friend's house after school. Frosty said gum lasted longer than candy and I could blow bubbles the whole way there. She remembered my birthdays with a shiny silver dollar, and she knew when I made my first communion or when I lost a tooth. I'm sure Frosty must've felt sick some days, or dreaded standing in the freezing winter wind. But for all the years I attended Hatch Elementary School, I don't remember her ever missing a single day of crossing guard duty.

It's amazing really to think what an impact she could make in the 15 steps it took to cross Ridgeland Avenue. No matter what happened, I knew Frosty would listen to my every word like there was nothing more important than hearing how my hamster got stuck in its Habitrail, or how I failed my multiplication tables for the eighth time. Frosty always knew just what to say. By the time I reached the other side of the street, my spirit felt lighter, and I believed in myself again. Even in my dreams to write.

Of course, I knew deep down that Frosty gave the same kind of guidance and encouragement to all the other kids, especially the ones who walked out of their way just to cross at Frosty's intersection. She held her post for nearly 30 years and sometimes I'd see the older kids return with a report card in hand, or a shiny class ring, or even a letterman jacket. They'd wait on the corner, anxious to show Frosty their latest accomplishments, beaming like they were still seven years old. I didn't know it then. But one day, I'd return to that same corner myself. At seventeen. Proud to tell Frosty how I'd been elected Editor-in-Chief of the high school newspaper. Just like she always knew I would.

It's been almost 40 years since Frosty first walked me across Ridgeland Avenue. I'm not a shy school girl any longer. In fact, I've grown to achieve much success in my professional career and in my writing pursuits. Still, I have to wonder how much of this I owe to Frosty and to the encouragement she gave me at a fragile time when I needed it the most.

I never knew Frosty's real name. Never saw the color of her hair beneath her uniform cap. In fact, I never spent more than a few minutes crossing the road with her each day. Yet somehow, in the brevity of those moments, Frosty left a memory so enduring I cannot think of her today without feeling a lump in my throat. I can see her still. Arms outstretched. Eyes smiling. White gloves waving me across the road.

I'm sure Frosty knew back then, what I am only now discovering. That even in the slightest intersection of lives, there lies an opportunity to make a powerful difference. To listen. To love. And to change someone forever.

Previously published at Thin Threads

PEACE FOR JIMMY
By Paula Timpson

I was happy to be alone with my boyfriend;
Jimmy, just us, simple-
He has always loved animals,
And so to please him,
I became open to us having a dog-
Jimmy adopted a fun American Eskimo
And this dog taught us so much about courage love and trust.
Fritz became blind in his later years,
And as we watched him swim in the sea, he was courageous and free
As a puppy...Fritz truly lived a full life and we did too
Enjoying his tricks and his wisdom!
To love a dog, brings full hearts and to let a dog go,
Brings tears and strength and hope-
In the end, we had to let Fritz go.
We shared in this moment of pure timelessness
As we watched Fritz's little smile come,
And then we simply felt his pure Spirit pass on-
To this day, we feel thankful to have had shared life with our 'dear',
Beloved friend, Fritz.
I believe opening my heart to let him in,
Helped breathe joy and unforgettable friendship that nothing;
Not even time could ever take away.

THE REUNION
By Carolyn T. Johnson

My heart raced. I blinked back tears. My finger hovered over the doorbell next to the house numbers - 12 Hillard Road. I'd been faithfully mailing Christmas cards to that address for over 40 years yet it had been that long since I'd seen her.

I gathered my composure, shuffled the vase of a dozen long-stemmed red roses to my other hip and rang the bell. It seemed like an eternity before the white screen door finally opened, then there she stood, all four-feet-ten of her, white hair, glasses, her Sunday-best pearls and a huge grin. She threw out her arms and squealed, "I just can't believe it - after all these years - you are just as pretty as your picture."

We first met when I was a seventh-grader just back stateside from three long years in Germany as an Army brat. My parents had enrolled me in her Sunday school class at church. The first day, I wore a light pink skirt, a white, frilly blouse and my new hush puppies in hopes of fitting in. She saw me hesitate at the door, walked over, bent down, said hello and introduced me to her class. She made me feel right at home. We sat down in a circle and she put me right next to her while she read us stories from the Bible.

At the end of that school year, my Sunday school teacher announced she was moving to St. Louis. By then, I had made lots of friends but was sad she was leaving.

That following Christmas, I was surprised when I pulled an envelope out of the mailbox postmarked St. Louis. It was a Christmas card from my Sunday school teacher telling all about her adventures in her new hometown. I bet she did this for all her former students. I asked my mom if I could have a Christmas card and I addressed it to Mr. and Mrs. Howard Moulding, 12 Hillard Road.

My birthday rolled around the following March. Again, I got mail postmarked St. Louis. I quickly ripped it open. She had signed it "Love, Mrs. Moulding." I was thrilled she had remembered but every Sunday school teacher probably sent her past school kids' birthday cards.

The tradition of exchanging cards continued over the years. I had no idea when Mrs. Moulding's birthday was but she never forgot mine. When she was younger, I would get handmade Christmas cards constructed out of bits and pieces of my previous year's card to her.

Sometimes she would send handmade bookmarks. In our cards, we would always write a note about what had happened over the past year.

I moved numerous times over the years and even changed last names several times but she never failed to find me. She always had words of encouragement to offer no matter what my circumstances. Whether I was switching majors, getting laid off from work, receiving a promotion, going through a divorce or getting remarried, she always believed in me.

As I got older, I wondered what she looked like. I had sent her several pictures of me but she never sent one in return. I once mailed her a little girl figurine holding a bouquet of flowers that reminded me of her. She sent a sweet thank you note with a picture of the figurine atop a doily but she was nowhere to be seen. When her husband passed away, I had to address her card to Mrs. Howard Moulding. I didn't even know her first name. She was always Mrs. Moulding to me.

"I can't believe it's been 40 years Mrs. Moulding," I said, as I pulled out her chair for her at the neighborhood restaurant.

"Call me Hester," she said, but it just didn't feel right. It seemed disrespectful to call her by her first name. I still felt like that little seventh-grader sitting beside her in the circle.

The waitress ran down the list of today's specials but said the soup was terrible. When she asked Mrs. Moulding for her order, the waitress was shocked when she said, "And I'll have some of that terrible soup to start," winking at me. I had to laugh. This lady had spunk. No wonder she piqued my interest as a child.

"So do you keep up with all the kids you used to teach?" I asked after ordering my salad. She said she exchanged cards with one other boy for a long time but doesn't hear much from him anymore. She used to write to a lot of her students but I'm the only one now.

I beamed, "You know you are the reason I got involved in the mentoring program for kids charities. I want to give back what you gave me. You were someone I could always count on to be on my side." She smiled, happy she had had such a positive influence on me.

Over dessert, I told Mrs. Moulding how I now watch for her card in the mail and worry when it's late. She laughed and said, "Dear child, don't worry about me. I know I won't be around forever. In fact, I've recorded the song I want played at my funeral. Would you like to hear it?"

As she warbled out the song of a life well-lived, tears well up in my eyes. I could picture her lying in her casket while her voice rang out loud and clear over the speakers. It broke my heart.

When the bill came, she insisted on splitting the tab but I would have none of it. It was my treat to get to spend time with her, to get to know her as an adult.

When we arrived back at her house, she invited me in. Her home was a cluttered testament to her long life. She walked me into her little kitchen and pointed out my wedding picture on her refrigerator. She then led me to the little table holding the figurine I had given her so many years ago.

I asked her about the hand-painted pictures leaning up against the wall. "Oh, those are ones I painted that didn't sell at the flea market. Would you like to see the rest?" she asked.

We crawled down the steep stairs to the basement. I was worried about her falling but she maneuvered them like she'd walked them a million times.

I found a winter scene with a lazy stream winding its way along the snow-covered bank, a leafless tree framing the left side of the picture and a red barn at the top of the hill. I loved it and wanted to buy it. She insisted that I take it although she was not happy that I chose the only one with no glass in the picture frame. It didn't matter. I was thrilled to have a little piece of her to take home with me.

Now when I look at that painting, I always think of the wonderful, wise, selfless woman who mentored me through the hills and valleys of my life. Although Mrs. Moulding is no longer around, for me, she will always be just a heartbeat away.

FOR MATTIE J. T. STEPANEK
By Justin Blackburn

Your heart song is my heart song
You proved to the world
No matter what happens you always belong
Through hardships as long as you understand God is the captain,
You can swim the sea, smile the sun, stay strong,
And inspire people like me.

Your imagination brings fairies to my eyes
Riding unicorns to my soul
Your hope for peace is my hope for peace
You knew heaven when you were only seven
You would not cease to show that peace
To the people asleep in their hopes and dreams

You illustrated to everyone how time does not control true love
You lived more in your short life then most dream of
You knew your love like the sun knows love
You gave beautiful acceptance to everyone
Because you felt God's beauty from inside

My friend I do not think twice
I feel you in heaven
I know you hear my prayers every night
Which makes me satisfied to sleep, to dream,
Knowing you are pain-free flying from star to star
With your perpetual angel wings

I love you,
Thank you for everything you taught me

MARC'S GRANDFATHER
What my son taught me about recovering from grief
By Rosalie Ferrer Kramer

When my father died, my children were quite young. Iris was eight, and she understood that she was never going to see her grandfather again. Danny was just three and didn't ask many questions; but my eldest son, Marc, who was six years old, was completely bewildered. He couldn't seem to figure out what had become of his beloved grandfather, whom he called Poppie.

My mother and father were in the habit of visiting in the evening, frequently arriving after dinner so they could participate in the nightly bedtime baths and story ritual. When my mother began to come alone, Marc would look behind her and question her, "Where is my Poppie? Why doesn't he come with you anymore?" All our clumsy explanations left him teary and more confused.

One night, several weeks after my father's death, my mother arrived late. I was already the bathroom with Marc and Danny in the tub. When she sat down on the toilet seat to keep us company, Marc asked the inevitable questions and she began to cry.

"Oh Grams, you must be lonesome," sympathized Marc.

"Yes I am," she replied wetly.

"You don't have a husband and I don't have a Poppie anymore," mused Marc.

A few moments later, his eyes lit up, and smiling with satisfaction, he said, "You know Grams, when I grow up, I'm going to marry you. Then you won't be lonely, and I'll have a grandpa again."

Our tears turned to laughter with his last remark. Mother felt better, and so did I. It was the first time either of us laughed out loud since my father's death. Muscular Dystrophy took Marc at the age of 22, but his words, uttered when he was a little boy, taught me that you can laugh and go on with your life after losing a loved one.

LIE IN FEAR
By Elsie Valentine

I first met Andrew just weeks after starting my freshman year in college. I walked into the small "green room" of our campus theatre and saw him surrounded by a group of students. He was a senior and the property master for our school's latest production, and I was assigned to his crew.

As I took my seat among the other students, the rest of the world quickly faded away. I can honestly say I don't remember anything other than his wavy brown hair and piercing blue eyes. I was smitten immediately.

Over the next few weeks, Andrew and I spent a lot of time together. Finding the props we needed for the show was like going on a treasure hunt. Our moments of fun and frustration were punctuated with nervous smiles, soulful stares, and the occasional soft good-bye kiss.

We had become friends – sometimes awkward friends – never really knowing if our relationship was platonic or romantic. We spent the rest of the school year dancing on a fine line between friends and lovers; but whenever things got a little too hot to handle, we both pulled away.

We were like one of those television couples brimming with sexual tension. You always hope they will get together, but their fear or stupidity manages to keep them apart.

To complicate matters, Andrew had an on-again, off-again girlfriend, and my insecurities never let me forget it.

As spring arrived and his graduation approached, our relationship came to a head. I had walked him to his car one afternoon when he asked me – point blank -- if my feelings for him were romantic or platonic. I was shocked by his directness and was taken completely off-guard. I knew my feelings were romantic, but I thought that answer would scare him away. I knew it scared me. So I lied and said platonic.

He accepted my answer without question then got in his car and drove away. I thought I had said the right thing; the answer that would keep him in my life after graduation, but it turned out to be the last time we saw each other.

It wasn't long before school was out and I was kicking myself for my cowardice. This wasn't just a matter of losing someone special anymore; it was about me letting my fear come between me and my heart's desire. I let my fear of failure – or fear of success – stop me from having something I really wanted. I robbed us of what we should have shared – an emotionally honest relationship.

A lot has happened in the many years since – some wonderful things – but I still find myself haunted at times by the thought of what might have been if I'd only had the strength and courage to be honest back then.

I don't know how he would have reacted to my true answer or how long we might have lasted, but I do know that everything that happened after my "platonic" response was based on a lie.

Since then, I learned that fear is like the boogeyman in the closet. It is only as big and dark and scary as your imagination makes it, and no more. I also learned that your hopes and dreams must always triumph over fear; otherwise you will spend the rest of your life wondering, "What if…" And finally, I learned that I never again want to lie in fear.

THE BLESSINGS OF A DEAR HEART
By Jeanine L. DeHoney

The pain in my belly was excruciating. I could hardly stand that day in February. The only thing I could do was call 911 and ask for an ambulance to take me to the hospital. I thought when I went to the emergency room that they would prescribe some pain killers and send me home with instructions to see my doctor, but a few hours turned into ten days of being in the hospital. A CAT scan revealed that a portion of my large intestine had twisted and I needed an operation to remove it.

I was petrified. I had just resigned from my job of 25 years to start a new one which was supposed to begin the following week. I had used all of my sick and vacation days and my husband and I were already struggling to pay a hefty mortgage. Overwhelmed by it all I asked out loud, "God why did you give me this cross to bear now?"

Late evening, I was moved to a hospital room on the seventh floor. After a restless night, I was awakened by doctors doing their early morning rounds. I overheard one doctor tell my roommate, whom I hadn't yet met because her curtain was closed, "There is nothing else we can do for you. We've talked to your sister and she decided that it would be best if you went to a hospice, Marge*."

My heart ached for this woman I had yet to meet. Minutes passed and I heard the hospital food cart screeching down the hallway, stopping momentarily in front of our room to bring us breakfast. Marge who had been very quiet was now humming a hymn and from the sounds she was making, thoroughly enjoying the food she was eating. I wondered how she come she wasn't inconsolable over her situation. She was told that there was nothing else that could be done to keep her alive. A family member was abandoning her to live in a place full of strangers. How could one find serenity or joy when this was handed to them?

After a while she got up, looked at me and smiled. "Hello dear heart, my name is Marge."

"I'm Jeanine," I said. She was a frail looking older woman in her late sixties but with an angelic and vibrant face.

Between a string of visitors that morning, both mine and hers, we didn't talk much to each other until after they left. I was still waiting for my scheduled operation. I eventually learned that Marge had pancreatic cancer. It was because she was a faith-filled woman that nothing or no one could daunt her.

Marge began praying for me. I was touched. At night when I was extremely restless because of the pain, she would sing a hymn to me. She had the voice of an angel and it lulled me to sleep like a lullaby, making me remember my own mother who if she was alive would have done the same.

On the day of my operation, Marge prayed for me again. "Dear God, please let my dear heart Jeanine come through this operation okay and make a full recovery."

Thankfully, my operation was successful but I was still in a lot of pain. Marge would often get up at night to get a nurse for me if they didn't answer me right away when I needed pain medication.

One morning, while I was drifting in and out of sleep, I heard Marge's doctor inform her that she would be leaving to go to the hospice the next morning. That evening, as she packed her belongings, she sang her hymns as happy as ever. I wanted to tell her how much I admired her strength and her care towards me. I wanted to tell her that she too was a dear heart, but I was in too much pain to speak that night or the morning of her departure.

When the nurse brought the wheelchair into the room for Marge, I tried to will myself to talk but still couldn't. Marge touched my hand tenderly as she was being pushed past my bed and said, "Everything will be okay, dear heart." All I could do was squeeze her hand back.

I was in the hospital for a few more days before I was discharged. I was going home but I was scared. I was still in a lot of pain and was not ready to leave – but then I thought of Marge.

Marge left going to a hospice like a joyous warrior. With a splash of red lipstick on her lips, she left not feeling defeated but feeling glorious. I had to do the same. I owed that to her, my waiting family and most of all myself.

Marge had lived a life of purposely not letting the sentence of pancreatic cancer curb her joy, her laughter, her praise or her love of wearing red lipstick. She chose to marvel at the roses and not worry about the thorns.

I watched how each day she chose the items on her menu, meticulously, slowly, as if it was a conscious thought and how she wouldn't let them take her tray until she had finished eating it all, thankful for her nourishment from God's bounty and the workers who prepared it. I listened to her sing hymns like a faith-filled songbird gracing me with a song each morning. I listened to her steadfast prayers that included my name. "Dear heart" and I will never forget the fragrant sound of it.

It's been over two years since my operation, and although I am still dealing with health problems, I often picture Marge putting on that red lipstick to greet the world and I push myself to do the same. I have so much to be thankful for, so many people who love me and I them, so many projects to get off the ground from writing a bestseller to putting stacks of photos in an album.

Wherever she is now, on earth still singing hymns or in Heaven singing with the angels, I hope she knows that she was indeed a dear heart herself, a beautiful tapestry woven with the finest threads of inspiration and compassion and a zest for life who inspired me to make each moment, each day, even those days that are on the side of cloudy, meaningful with a splash of elation or what I like to call red lipstick.

Her name has been changed

BEND
For my friend Catherine
By Lisa Miles

You maneuvered your chair through doors closed by ignorance,
into rooms darkened by the unenlightened and the unduly privileged
And you were instructed by some, who served as our village idiots
but you succeeded, and you did more,
You opened doors that were closed before
You were mindful of the disability of others,
including deficiencies in me
And you shared your own kind of therapy
For me, that meant learning to bend
From the waist down, and to look around at the world from your view
But more than that,
I had to learn to bend my mind too
I needed to really get to know you,
I needed to know that you are so much more
then the limitations that I first saw
You knew all along that the only handicap that would stand between us
Would be mine, not yours,
And you made reasonable, and not so reasonable accommodations,
And exercised an amazing amount of patience
But you taught me, and so many others, how to bend
And that is the most beautiful, amazing, unselfish gift
You can ever give to a friend.

AN ANGEL UNAWARE
"One family's dysfunction is another family's teacher."
By Diana M. Amadeo

I first met Pauly in October at the city's ice skating rink. While my daughter struggled into skates before her very first lesson, the unshaven man in soiled tattered clothes ambled over, told an unintelligible joke and laughed before I could react.

My first thought was that Pauly was a homeless man who had sought refuge inside the public building. His physical appearance and style of speech was suggestive of life as a social outcast. But despite first impressions, there was something very safe in his demeanor. Surrounding his four feet ten, rotund physique, was a childlike aura. Pauly was one of those few adults who had surpassed middle-age, yet still retained a chubby, gaped-tooth innocence with a smile that filled his entire face.

Soon, it became apparent that he was, indeed, employed by the rink. But just what his job description was remained obscure. Eager to talk, but finding few who would pay attention, I quickly became an ally just by the art of listening. In no time at all, he began to look forward to our weekly excursions to the rink. Sometimes he would wait for us, gentlemanly open the door and proceed to ramble about his day. Before I could decipher the gist of his message, he would begin to laugh heartily at his own words.

Over the five years that my daughter took ice skating lessons, Pauly revealed that he lived with his aged mother in the city. He had a married brother who lived in the adjoining town along with several nieces and nephews. Despite the close proximity to his relatives, it seemed they didn't include him much in their activities. Because he was, well, different.

But to Pauly, these skaters were more than kin. They were his friends. He'd talk to them all...and didn't take offense if they walked away with no response. There wasn't a mean bone in his body. He was gentle and harmless, always greeting people with a big smile. Even to those who returned an eternal scowl.

Then, one week, there was no one to greet us at the door. I was immediately concerned, but then breathed a sigh of relief when he approached me in the rink. But this day, Pauly was very sullen. "I got some bad news this morning," he said with a quivering voice. "I found out that a good friend of mine had an asthma attack and died." His face contorted. He began to sob.

"She had some problems during the night, but her parents thought she was okay. They woke up this morning and found her blue; by the time the ambulance got her to the hospital she was dead. My good friend died. My friend died."

As I listened to Pauly, rubbed his back and listened some more, I suddenly became very chilled. He was talking about one of his kin...one of his friends...one of the child skaters in the session before my daughter's. He grieved for his good friend, one of the kids that rarely acknowledged him.

The following week, Pauly greeted us at the door of the ice skating rink as his jolly self. Then he teared up as he spoke of the young girl's funeral. As he talked, it was easy to envision this broken man at prayer alone in the back of the church. It seemed through his private spiritual communion, that Pauly became revitalized, renewed and reborn.

It was then that I realized how truly special this man was. His simplicity and humility helps him let go of all the negativity from people who keep him at a distance. Instead of focusing on the daily rejections, he holds each person he meets close to his heart. Any person who is fortunate enough to meet Pauly receives from him pure grace – unconditional love – a profound love that is not contingent upon its return.

To meet Pauly is to greet an angel unaware. A true friend.

LIFE IS WHAT IT IS
In Memory of Randy Pausch, author: The Last Lecture
By Belinda Sue

From the day
    We're born.
To the moment
    We die.
"Life is what it is."
    We learn to live between the lines.

Whether it's an illness
    We survive.
Or the death
    Of love we fear.
"Life is what it is."
    No matter, what you hold dear.

We all must go
    Through life phases.
Living our life,
    Until the day we die.
"Life is what it is."
    The end is our true demise.

I will take the day,
    With gratitude.
My experiences
    Will tell me why.
"For life is what it is."
In this...
    My Lesson Lies.

LASTING LESSONS FROM A LITTLE SISTER
By Ysabel de la Rosa

After living in an assortment of far-away cities, I returned to my home town, looking for a job. In one interview, the CEO said, "Your sister does such great work in our community!" "Yes," I said, "but I'm older and I taught her everything she knows." He laughed. It was funny. But it wasn't completely true.

I *was* older, but I certainly didn't teach my sister "everything she knew." The truth was, she taught me many things, even as a toddler. We were as different as night and day—and as irrevocably connected. I was serious and introverted. She was bubbly and a natural performer. She had honed a Louis Armstrong voice by age three and could get any neighborhood child to join her Fourth of July sunrise parades. I buried myself in books while she sat in front of the television, empathizing with the characters of *Days of Our Lives*. I carried crayons and paper from room to room; she, her tool belt, ready to start a "project."

I sang in the church choir, but never braved a solo. My sister made up her own songs and shared them with anyone at a moment's notice. My favorite one: "Oh, Lord, you drive me crazy, but I'm not gonna blame it on you!" An excellent faith doctrine, if I ever heard one. She taught me to hammer a nail; when we sang in choirs together, she kept me on pitch.

Once asleep, I slept heavily. My sister slept lightly and awoke one dawn to alert my mother to smoke coming from a fire in our basement. The three-year-old in the green robe saved our lives. This taught me a lasting sense of wonder at close calls and the grace of saving moments.

She was an unpredictable mixture of practicality and joy. I, on the other hand, was emotional first and practical a distant second. Our grandparents came every Christmas for two weeks. At visit's end, our grandfather always gave each of us a crisp dollar bill—quite a sum in the 1960s for little girls. Payday notwithstanding, I would cry when our grandparents were about to leave. The family made fun of me, so once I hid behind a door, thinking no one would see my tears. My nosy little sister found me and said cheerfully, "Don't cry! We're getting a dollar!" A practical observation, yet expressed with joy—a combination that has personified her throughout her life.

While our personalities remained distinctively different into adulthood, we shared deep values, including a profound love for family. During our mother's 13-year illness, which disabled her beyond anything we could have imagined, my sister and I would lend each other strength and humor when we needed it most. Our parents lived in a historic home, and our mother always said no to frequent requests to include our home in house tours. We were never sure why, but she always said no. Two years after she died, our father said yes to the tour organizers.

Three days before the tour, a raccoon crawled under the house and died. The stench was foul, acrid, pervasive and sharp. My sister and I set out to purchase air sanitizers, fresheners, candles — anything we could find to conquer that odor. As we stood beneath fluorescent lights in Wal-Mart, the same thought struck each of us: our mother was jinxing the tour! We laughed so hard, we doubled over; air wicks and sprays bunched in our hands. The humor could be shared only by the two of us: we had not forgotten her suffering by any means, but we clearly remembered her steel magnolia spirit and indomitable will. We were *almost* getting by with something of *almost* cosmic proportions.

When I moved abroad without thinking through all the consequences, my sister sent me practical presents, things I needed but could no longer afford. (A needed gift is much more valuable than a wanted one.) She visited me once in Spain and kindly and honestly told me how she saw circumstances affecting me there. When I needed to flee that foreign situation, she paid my plane ticket home.

When our father died, she helped me navigate my way through the grief and the years of sorting through the estate of the strong and gentle man who taught us to tie shoelaces, ride bikes, and look up words in dictionaries. There were times, too, when she turned to me and, I hope, I was the help she needed. I turned to her more often, though. I often told people I was fortunate to have a sibling who was a younger and older sister in one.

Because she was younger, I never, and I do mean *never*, contemplated the possibility that she would leave this earthly plane before me. When she called to tell me that the CT scan revealed that the cancer had spread to her liver, I responded to the tremor in her voice with a fierceness in my own. "We will fight this," I said. But this time, the serious and bubbly, emotional and practical sisters were no match for the circumstances. The tumors were fueled by aggressive neuro-endocrine cells. A rare and dangerous bleeding condition developed, preventing chemotherapy. Surgery corrected the bleeding, but by the time she recovered from surgery, the tumors had consumed nearly 80 percent of her liver.

My sister looked at the oncologist with clear, blue eyes and asked, "So, there's nothing more to be done?" The oncologist regretted it deeply, but the answer was "No, nothing more." The doctor left the room. I reached for my sister's hand.

"I don't want to be here without you," I said. "And, I'm not ready to go," she replied. "But, I can make my peace with it."

I know that is true. Her deep spiritual practice and enlightened Christian faith give her the resources to find that peace, as does her life of "good works." She has sown joy everywhere she has lived and worked: as the city employee who would work 60 or more hours a week to see a community project to fruition; the church member who volunteered to be youth leader when no one else would; the lyrical Sister Robert Anne in *Nunsense* and the enticing Marlene Dietrich at musical fundraisers. I know her good works blanket this part of the world, a world she has consistently turned into a better place for others.

Still, I find myself in unmapped territory. I've never faced a loss or crisis without her. Yesterday, I sat by her hospital bed, tears in my eyes as dark and brown as hers are light and blue, and asked her: "How will I—what will I—do when you're not here?"

Her answer was swift and unwavering: "You'll keep being my big sister." Then she told me: What she wants for her funeral—no eulogy, much music. What she wants her savings account to do: start a scholarship, fund a historical restoration, support her church. What matters most: her family. "What do you want in place of a eulogy?" I asked. "I'm writing a letter," she said. "Someone can read it." Her eyes were dry—but by no means devoid of feeling or meaning. Those are strong, clear eyes, I thought, and there is elegant courage in that pale countenance. For a moment, my eyes, too, were dry, and I, too, felt braver, stronger—thanks to her.

She taught me to be practical, to pick myself up when I need to, to not drown in emotion. She showed me how to laugh at divine and necessary moments; how to walk with someone through everything life offers and everything it takes away. Now, she is teaching me how to die. It's the last lesson I ever wanted from her.

"None of us is promised tomorrow," she told me. Then she handed me a gift an eighth-grader from her church gave her. It said: "I don't know what tomorrow holds, but I know who holds tomorrow."

She touched my hand and said, "I'll still be around." My arm encircled her frail, thin body and I said, "I will find you."

She has only days left now, although no one knows how many. The truth is none of us knows the number of our days, and that one unknown fact should serve as guiding light, or guiding shadow, as the case may be.

I cannot contemplate a tomorrow without my sister. Yet, as I have so many other times, I can learn from her. I believe that learning from my sister—my brave, beautiful, bubbly and wise little sister—will be something I do until my days here are done and I go to discover what new songs she is singing, what new things she has to teach me, things just like her—made of heaven and of earth. Night and day. So different, and so irrevocably connected.

TRULY BLESSED
By Lynn C. Johnston

When I found more pain in others
Than I found within myself
I learned what it meant to feel compassion
And my pain began to fade

When I found more forgiveness in others
Than I found within myself
I learned what it meant to feel peace
And my heart began to mend

When I found more belief in others
Than I found within myself
I learned what it meant to have faith
And my fears began to die

And when I found more love in others
Than I found within myself
I learned what it meant to feel truly blessed
And my spirit began to soar

Previously published in
Angel's Dance: A Collection of Uplifting and Inspirational Poetry

WINSTON
By Judy Kirk

The first black man I ever knew
was the sexton at my church
when I was growing up.
He taught me Presbyterian rituals
and how to talk to God.

He did it as he swept the sidewalk,
never one to shirk his duties,
his appearance always neat and clean
white shirt, dark trousers and suspenders.
He reminded me of my Grandfather.
I could spot his familiar figure
blocks away and quickened my
step to reach him.

As he pushed that large rectangular broom
day after day, week after week,
we became friends.
I was never in a hurry to leave when Winston
was talking to me because he listened.

Even as young as I was
I felt his ease with God,
talking about Him as if he were
a close friend. He defined for me what a
relationship with God could be.

Everything about him was safe - his demeanor,
his words, his eyes. He was goodness
wrapped up like a loaf of freshly baked bread
and because of him, the ugliness of bigotry
perpetrated by my mother and others
who labeled people by their heritage,
never seeped into my heart.
He had swept it clean.

THE GREENHORN
By Florence Reiss Kraut

I met my father-in-law in the small, two-bedroom apartment in the Bronx, where he and his wife had raised their sons. He tried to hide his hands from me when I went to shake his. He told me later he was ashamed of the black grease line under his nails which, scrub as he might, he could not completely erase. He had a missing pointer finger on his right hand, which had been cut off by an errant elevator chain in a work accident. He wore a plaid flannel shirt and gray work trousers. He was six feet tall, and his hair, once blonde, was almost white, but still full. His blue eyes flashed, and he spoke English fluently, but with a heavy Yiddish accent. "I'm just a greenhorn," he said.

I was a newly minted college graduate with intellectual pretentions and sophisticated New York aspirations, two generations removed from Ellis Island and the grinding poverty which had forced my own grandparents to immigrate. I was a bit of a snob.

He said, "I don't speak so good. I have no education."

"That's all right," I stammered. "It doesn't matter." But I wondered. In the world I came from it mattered. My parents schooled us in classical music, in art, in theater and ballet. My mother was an artist, my father played bridge with world ranked players. I looked around this tiny apartment, at the spotless kitchen with its Formica table, scrubbed linoleum floor, and shiny percolator coffeepot bubbling away on the stove, at the living room with its worn sofa and I wondered. Papa called himself a greenhorn, and I guess I thought he was one too.

Then Allen and I went to Europe. It was the first time I had ever been out of the United States, the first time traveling to a country where a different language was spoken, the first time I had to think carefully before I asked for directions, starting sentences with, "Pardon, but do you speak English?"

I felt fine walking around with my new husband. It was a lark, finding our way to landmarks with our guidebooks and maps. But one afternoon, Allen had a prearranged business meeting in Paris, and I thought I would wander around on my own, just soaking up the atmosphere of this beautiful city. I had taken French in high school, and knew some rudimentary words. I would be fine.

I walked for a long time, mesmerized by everything I saw around me. And then it was time to meet Allen at the Hotel Marie Louise where we were staying. With a stab of anxiety I realized I had no idea what street it was on. I wanted to approach someone to ask for help, but I did not know how to explain my predicament in French. Today, the dilemma would be solved with a simple cell phone call, but then there were none. Something very near panic began to engulf me.

I stopped several people, and in butchered French I asked them if they had heard of the Hotel Marie Louise. Some stopped, then shrugged and walked away. Some didn't even bother to pause, but brushed by me. I looked for a policeman, but saw none. It finally occurred to me that a hotel, if I could find one, would have a concierge, a phone book, and help. Feeling very stupid, I made my way into the lobby of a hotel, and got the help I needed to find my hotel, its address and a taxi.

In the scope of things, it was not a very momentous experience. But it was a nudge, a reminder, and I stored it in my head to think about later, about how seeking help in a language you barely understand is not so easy.

I thought about my father-in-law. Not once, not twice, but four times, he had started over. He had reinvented himself, each time in a new language, a new country, a new occupation, stepping into different cultures, asking haltingly for work, eating strange food and making new friends, learning to read like a kindergarten child, again and again and again, everywhere a greenhorn, trying not to feel stupid.

I knew the outlines of Papa's life. He was 14 when he was sent from a small village in Lithuania to a town in Germany to apprentice as a mechanic at a distant relative's home. At 17, he was conscripted into the German army and drove an ambulance over brown and barren Russian war fields, shells whistling overhead and rutting the road. Then, in the grinding post-World War I depression in Germany when there was no work he migrated to Holland with a friend and there they talked themselves into jobs with a German steamship company, claiming they could work the steam engines, although they'd never done it before. They sailed to Central America learning the mechanics of steamships, cruising between the old and the new worlds and finally getting off in Vera Cruz, enticed by the prospect of helping build the railroads in Chihuahua, Mexico. I think of him there, for the next ten years, riding his horse, working in a new country, the cadences of his native Yiddish and his German, fading in his memory.

When he finally came to New York City to help his widowed sister his Yiddish was almost forgotten, he had not spoken it for so long. He had every intention of going back to Mexico but in New York he met a young woman who came from a village near his home, and they fell in love and married. He remade his life again, learning to install and repair elevators in Manhattan buildings, starting his own business, living in the small apartment in the Bronx and raising his two sons.

His was the quintessential American immigrant story, not that different from many others, but I was intrigued by it. Growing up I had never thought much about how lucky I was to have been born in the United States. I took for granted my home, the food on the table, my free education, my car, my clothes, my comfort. Still, I didn't really understand until one stormy November day. My mother-in-law was sick and Papa telephoned and asked me to come to stay with her while he went to vote.

"It's so nasty out," I said. "It's not so terrible if you miss this time. It's only a mid-year election."

His voice shook with indignation. "I will vote. Every year I vote. I don't miss because of rain. If you don't come I'll find another way."

I came. He went out into the rain and returned with his dripping umbrella, sat down at the kitchen table and over coffee talked and talked about where he came from, what it was like being an outsider, not belonging, spilling pain and loss and memories. "Here, I belong," he said. "I may be a greenhorn, but I have the same right as you." His eyes blazed, and I was ashamed of myself. He reached across the table, took my hand and said, "You go home and vote." I did.

I remember my father-in-law now as one of the proudest citizens I knew. I see him arguing politics vigorously, reading the New York Post every day from cover to cover. He adopted every American custom he could, watching the baseball games his sons played, leading their Boy Scout troops, taking them for hiking and camping trips in upstate New York. After World War II he went to Washington as an American citizen to sponsor his wife's cousins who survived the Holocaust, so they could come into the United States and resurrect their lives.

My father-in-law, Paul Kraut, was a simple man. He drove an old car, lived in small apartments in the Bronx, went to Orchard Beach with folding chairs, cheese sandwiches and a thermos of coffee and stared out at the gray Atlantic Ocean remembering where he had come from. He did not have much money, but he knew who he was. He was a successful man.

When he was about 80 years old, his eyes had clouded with cataracts and macular degeneration; he could no longer drive a car and he walked with a cane. One day, when I had brought him to our home in the suburbs, he was climbing the stairs to our front door, leaning heavily on the banister, and I took his arm to help him.

He shook my hand away. "Don't make me an invalid!"

At first I was offended. But then I realized that his pushing me away was a symbol of his strength. He had survived and succeeded by struggling and pushing forward with every ounce of energy, always trying, never giving up. He taught that lesson to his sons, who in turn passed it to their children. And I, who learned the lesson later in life, now carry it in my heart.

ROLE MODEL
By Mary Elizabeth Laufer

You called a room with a desk your *office*,
You didn't submit your poems, you *marketed* them.
You made the business of writing poetry sound as respectable
as any nine-to-five skirt-and-suit-jacket job.

You ignored the snide put-downs, the belittling remarks,
"That and fifty cents will get you a cup of coffee...,"
the worst offender our own father,
his little jabs deflected by your wit.

From you I learned I didn't need his permission
to put pen to paper, only my own.
You convinced me that what we wrote mattered;
our words bore witness to the lives of all women.

Years later we read our poems before an audience,
and Dad was there, an old man, shrunken and gray.
I heard no snickers or jeers from him that night.
He simply listened and clapped.
I think he was proud of his daughters, really proud.

BUBBA'S LESSONS
By Beckie A. Miller

In Bubba's world life was simple. He only needed a full tummy, love and hugs, his clown or Richard Simmons' videos to watch on television and his basic care needs met. Some people are almost fearful of dealing with the special and perpetual children of the world – of understanding he was simply a child in an adult body and accepting that child just as he was. He always wanted to say "Hi" and shake everyone's hand that he met. Some willingly would take his hand but many others shied away, as if whatever he had might prove to be contagious.

I believe those like Bubba are sent here to teach us many life lessons, but the most important one being *unconditional love*. Bubba loved everyone. If you simply smiled or shook his hand you were his friend for life and it mattered not who you were, the color of your skin, what you had accomplished, your station in life – just that you were you.

He was born in 1972 with cerebral palsy, a cleft pallet, and the inner parts of his ears undeveloped. With a hearing aid he could hear but not well enough to learn to speak succinctly. He had an extra thick tongue which forced him to breathe through his mouth and eat noisily but no one knew at birth what the extent of his mental functions would be. He did not walk until he was eight, and only after corrective surgeries to help his tangled legs. Then doctors said he would only walk temporarily and be crippled again. He showed them up on that one, still walking more than 20 years later, although using the wheel chair more and more. He may not have walked easily or great distances, but he could sure make a quick trip to the refrigerator when he wanted to get something!

Before 1996 when my sister-in-law Sonya moved to Phoenix from Georgia with Bubba, into the guest house on our property, I knew of Bubba but really did not know him. As I watched my nephew and grew close to him, I came to realize no one need feel sorry for his life. In fact, I was envious at times of the simplicity of his life – his physically-challenged version of Peter Pan, remaining a child forever. It was his life; and if all of us remained more childlike and appreciative of the simple, little things in our adult lives, life would be more meaningful and full of joy as Bubba's was -- without great expectations and all the trappings and frustrations of the adult world.

Bubba loved to eat – one of his great pleasures in his simple world. He loved even the stuff he was allergic to, which ended up being a lot. When they moved here from Georgia, they began sharing many family meals with us. Bubba loved his Aunt Beckie's cooking, but he ended every single meal rambunctiously thanking his Uncle Don. He never once thanked me, his aunt and the chef, for dinner. We used to joke about it and how I liked to think he was thanking his Uncle Don for marrying his Aunt Beckie, who was such a good cook!

And his Clowns. Oh, how Bubba loved clowns. Every time he saw one he screamed with excitement, cupping his nose with his fingertips, his sign language for clown. I remember we took him to Las Vegas one year and stayed intentionally at Circus Circus Hotel just so he could enjoy all the clowns. For the first time with Bubba, eating was not the first on his list to do; he wanted to see the clowns all the time. His Uncle Don had to tell him – "Eat first, clowns later" to calm him down and allow us to do anything else while there. He repeated that same phrase many times since that trip years ago, his way of remembering something unforgettably special for him. We made other trips together, to the Grand Canyon for one, and it was always nicer to view the world with Bubba's joyful abandon through the eyes of innocence and youthful appreciation.

Bubba also had a thing for bathrooms. He had to scope out the bathroom anywhere we went even when he did not have to use it. I think his cousin, my grandson Dillon, inherited that from Bubba. He loves to do the same thing. I never figured out why and what he was looking for in each bathroom, but Bubba must have enjoyed it or was searching for something in each.

Then, one morning, Sonya called me to say Bubba had been admitted to the hospital with pneumonia. When I got to the hospital he had already been transferred from a regular ward to Intensive Care. I walked into his room hearing first his struggle to breathe and the constant hiss of the oxygen tank. Bubba was asleep. I did not realize then he would never wake up again due to two massive brain strokes and some smaller ones from an infection that spread rampantly in his body.

Each year since 1996, I have searched the stores and magazines continuously trying to find him something with clowns for birthdays and Christmas and yet something different that he did not already have. I know I still will do it even now that he is gone, his tired body giving up the great fight, as Bubba will always be a part of my heart and clowns will forever be what brings him to mind. I cannot look at a clown without remembering his absolute joy for them.

During those last days of hospitalization and tons of tests, we learned more about Bubba's health condition than ever before. We learned he had already lived 10 to 15 years longer than most with his degree of disabilities. We also learned what a truly walking miracle he had been all his life when the radiologist who saw his MRI was absolutely amazed the degree of function Bubba did manage to have because he was really living with very little brain matter. That radiologist had assumed he had only lived in a vegetative state until Bubba's family doctor corrected him. Just goes to show you how much you can do with *heart* matter. And Bubba had a whole lot of heart.

Bubba left his tired, worn out body and joined the angels, but I believe that angels surrounded Bubba his entire life. He was here to teach an important lesson of unconditional love and more. I am so glad to have had him a part of our family and a part of my life. His simple joy for life lives on in me, especially when I face tough times or forget to draw on the inner child deep inside my adult self. Always remember that child in each of us. Children are not tainted by life's hardness. They do not feel prejudice only acceptance. They laugh whole-heartedly and without abandon as Bubba did. They believe in miracles. We all need to do this and live our life with joy.

Esmond Lee "Bubba" Turbyfield
October 8, 1972 – April 16, 2008

SELF PORTRAIT
By Robin Brown

    When I was ten, I sat at the kitchen table with my grandmother. She looked at me through the smoke curling out of the end of her cigarette; she took a long drag and then sighed out excess letting it linger in her age. Reaching across the table, she grabbed my hand and out of nowhere she said, "Robin, you will never ever be pretty, but you will always be attractive and that is more important." I wanted to slap her, I wanted to yell at her and tell her how much that had hurt me; but instead I pouted and we didn't speak to each other for the rest of the day. It's funny how much our loved ones see even before we do.

    A very close friend of mine is a photographer and had recently asked me to pose for her. At first I had laughed it off telling her to go find some pretty little girl to pose for her if she wanted them to be something worth looking at. She persisted so I finally gave in, in lieu of this project and set up an appointment to do a shoot with her. I didn't expect to take off my clothes but once we started it seemed only natural. I mean what better way to get a look at you, without all the daily camouflage. It was quite possibly one of the most intense experiences I have ever been a part of; we took a total 784 pictures that night. It took her a week to print out the best ones from the contact sheets. It took me another week to grow the balls to look at them. Halfway through them I started crying, not because they were bad, but because I had never imagined myself being able to be a part of something so beautiful. That is the reminder of me, from the first conscious breath I take. I am my insecurities, I am my imperfections; I never thought that an experience like that one has been would have shown me what others have seen for a long time. It's given me the perspective that we are all art, and that our features shape our character and are only a matter of circumstance.

    The first thing that struck me were the colors – blue to most represents cold or ice, but in truth when a flame burns to its potential, it burns blue almost white. So much of my skin in this is blue or white, which is to say a cool exterior doesn't mean there's nothing burning on the inside. Next is the fact that I have a huge problem with my freckles, I always have – I used to think that they were breeding while I was asleep. Everyone tried to tell me that freckles were a unique feature; I never wanted to hear that from people with beautiful tanned skin. Now, I love the way they look more than ever because of these photos. They look like somebody air-brushed me all over; as if my skin were an artist's canvas and freckles were avant-garde. Every one of them is a perfectly positioned imperfection given to me by heredity and the love of the summer, I will pray in the sunlight with freckles as my rosaries. I will never tan but my skin will always be bejeweled with the remembrance of warmth.

We all have those parts that we wish we could change; I guess if I had to make up my mind about one it would have to be my nose. It's big and crooked and has a hump in the middle of it; like my forehead was going too fast so they had to install a speed bump. My grandmother told me, "It gives you character." I thought she was a liar; but I do believe that I wouldn't be me without it and sometimes see my nose out of the corner of my eye and remember not to take my face so seriously. The more I look at it, the more I think my face is trying to keep up with the rest of my body; its curves remind me that I can look interesting in certain lights.

I don't have dainty little girl hands, they're cut and scarred and sometimes they don't make sense, but they are the hands born to a family of hard workers. I know the value of getting them dirty, I know the value calluses and the way scars have a way of speaking through the skin. I know the neurosis behind bitten fingernails, the passion between palms and the secret language of fingertips; translating emotion into another's soul. The creases and caverns of my hands are highways into a Frost future, and prove that all roads lead inward. The tiny pieces of silver that decorate the space between my knuckles remind me of how close a person can stay, even after they're gone.

This is me, balanced in between what I expect of myself and what the rest of the guests on this planet expect. I will never be pretty; those words have resonated behind my eyes for so long, oftentimes stealing the glory and beauty of what I really am. It took me 13 years and my grandmother's passing to finally understand what she had meant that morning at the table. Realizing that I had completely disregarded the last part of what she had told me all those years before. That there was something behind imperfection that would leak out and show itself with pride to the world. It took losing myself to addictions, to loves, to periods of crazy freedom, to finally know that the face that sees me from the mirror each morning is not the face of a pretty girl. It's the face of a strong, capable, and attractive young woman. My eyes, my skin with its imperfections, my crooked nose and my ugly hands all tell a story every day. Today I saw past what image is; I saw my grandmother and smiled.

TWO LEFT SHOES
By E. Baker

When I am a girl
almost 11
my big brother
is mean to me
and lets me get
wrong shoes
for my feet

Back home
from the shoe store
off busy Victory Drive
he says, while laughing too,
what he tells me in the store:
They'll fit better later on
I watch his lie smile kind
of creep over his face
having his secret
joke at my dumbness
I do not yet know about

I see his car coming
down our yard, and
I rush —
I mean I fly —
to put on my
new red shoes
to show my daddy
I tell him, though,
as if I know something smart:
They hurt right now
but I add what my brother
already told me a time or two:
They'll fit better later on

Daddy flips . . .

At first I think
he just does not like red shoes
and I am about to cry
till he says
No, Baby, they won't ever fit
Don't cry
See . . .
they're two left shoes
They point away
from your little feet
They sold you two shoes
for your left foot
That's why they hurt and
point away from your feet

Boy, I asked
you to help your little sister
buy these shoes . . .
You didn't see they're wrong . . .

Amazed at us —
our innocence and
ignorance —
but still teaching
his little one
Daddy says:
You want a left one,
yes, you do just like you got
for your left foot
And you want a right one
for your right foot too
They will not point
away from each other
See, like mine . . .

I see his do not

Let me have them . . .
and the box
Daddy grabs the shoes
Come on, he says to me,
'cause he sees

I still do want my red shoes
For sure, we're off
to the shoe store
where no one dares resist
what he demands

a proper fitting pair of
5 AA red shoes
for my little girl

and says to everyone in the shoe store

You all sold my baby two left shoes

Me,
the rest of my life,
I love red shoes
heels, flats, boots
and more
I love my daddy
who teaches me
all things
without making me
feel stupid
and is the live example
for me
of how to stand up
for myself:

You want just one shoe
for your left foot
and one for
your right foot too...

MY PROVERBS 31 GRANDMOTHER
"A worthy woman who can find?
For her price is far above rubies." - Proverbs 31:10
By Francine L. Billingslea

My grandmother was one of the strongest women spiritually, physically, mentally and emotionally that I knew or think I'll ever know. My grandparents had 16 children – my mother being the second oldest. I was the first grandchild.

We always called the family home "Momma's house," mainly because it was Momma who ran the show. She was a devout Catholic and every child attended parochial school at some point and time in their lives. My grandmother was determined to give her children the educational opportunities that she didn't have. She spent a few hours, a few days a week doing domestic work and cleaning the convent and rectory to help make ends meet. Most of her pay went towards her children's tuition.

Momma made sure we were never without. The holidays I experienced as a child were the best I ever had, even to this day, and because the family was so big, there was big everything! A huge Easter basket, a turkey that looked like a baby dinosaur and the biggest Christmas tree they could find. Periodically, family photos were taken by a professional photographer and we always did family-oriented things, which were always done with class and taste. Even though my parents separated while I was a baby, because of Momma, I was still able to learn and experience family devotedness and its values and blessings.

What I remember most about my grandmother was how loving, nurturing, mild-mannered, giving, soft-spoken, reliable, and dependable she was. You could go to her for anything at any time and she would stop whatever she was doing and give you her undivided attention. Momma won "The Mother of the Year" award twice in her lifetime.

Last but not least, I remember the numerous times that I either saw or heard her praying. One day, I asked her why was she always praying and I'll never forget the answer. She said, "Because first of all, I always want to be humble and thank God for all he's done and given us. Second, I'm depositing prayers into my prayer bank because I don't know when my children, their seeds, or any of my loved ones might need to make a withdrawal and if they haven't put anything in. I don't want the family account to be empty." I said, "I don't understand." She smiled and said, "When you become a mother, you will." *"She opened her mouth with wisdom; and the law of kindness was on her tongue." Proverbs 31: 26.*

Momma was always sewing, hemming, washing, ironing, cooking, and cleaning, always with a smile and never without an apron. Every so often, she'd gather our shoes and take them to the shoe-makers to be resoled. Momma worked hard in and outside of the home, she was a devoted wife, mother, grandmother and a praying woman. She made and did the best she could with whatever she had, and it was always for her family. *"She looked well to the ways of her household." Proverbs 31:27.*

When my grandfather passed away, I remember during the wake and the funeral; I constantly kept an eye on Momma. Now when I look back, I know I saw deep pain, but I also saw strength through her dignified grieving manner. Momma was only 52 years old at the time. To me, she was an old lady, but in reality, she was still a young woman who stayed true to her first love until the time of her death ten years later. *"Strength and dignity are her clothes." Proverbs 31:25*

When I first got married back in the early seventies, Momma sat me down and gave me a few quick lessons about being a good wife and mother. However with the complexities of that era, I didn't implement all that I was taught and told. I quickly became a wife and mother with a demanding job and taxing hours outside of the home. God was on my list, but I didn't put him first. Soon I became a single parent heading down the wrong paths. I often thought about my grandmother and the kind of woman she was. As time went on, her examples helped me to get my life back on track.

As I matured, remarried, and became a grandmother myself, I began to try to be the kind of woman, wife, mother, and grandmother that Momma was. It wasn't long before I clearly understood why Momma was always praying. It's because we truly need God in our lives for help, guidance, wisdom, true peace, and happiness. And yes, we need to sincerely intercede for our loved ones.

Times have drastically changed since my grandmother had and raised her children, and I'm sure it was just as hard for her back then as it is for mothers now. But what I've come to realize over the years is, the reason why my grandmother was the way she was. It was because she kept her priorities in order; she stayed focused on God and her wifely and motherly duties – and not on a career, fashions, fortune, or the "in" things of her time. She was a committed woman who was sincere, dedicated, and loyal. Through it all, she remained focused on her commitments.

Even now when I get upset or despondent, I think about my grandmother and what she undoubtedly endured, accepted, or tolerated and never complained about, I become encouraged and reinvigorated.

She was truly an exceptional, a unique, a one-of-a-kind woman, and definitely a role-model with a hard act to follow. *"A woman that fears God shall be praised."* Proverbs 30:31

What did I learn from this woman? I learned strong morals and values and how to love and respect myself as well as others. I learned the significance of true love, honesty and commitment. I learned how to work hard in and outside of the home and still take care of my family. I learned how to recognize my need for God and prayer and put them first. I learned how to act like a lady and be a woman in every sense of the word.

These qualities were handed down to my mother, who handed them down to me. I handed them down to my daughter and she is now handing them down to her children.

I, as well as other family members who have fallen by the wayside at one time or another, still remember Momma and give her credit for helping us to get back on the straight and narrow – even long after her passing.

It is because of her that most of us sent our children to parochial schools. It is because of her that morals, values, and traditions of old are not forgotten and instilled. It is because of her that we try to be the best women, mothers, grandmothers, and wives that we can be. It is because of her that we try to keep our families together, work hard in and outside of the home and make the best with and what we have, and it is because of her that we know about making prayer deposits and are still making withdrawals from her account. *"Her children rise up and call her blessed."* Proverbs 31:28

None of us women in the family can call each other a Proverbs 31 woman, but we sure can say we had a good example. When I think of my mother and the kind of woman she was, when I look at my daughter and see the kind of woman she's turned out to be, and when I look back over my life, I tearfully look up and first, I thank God and then I thank Momma. We don't have a choice but to be strong women spiritually, physically, mentally and emotionally because our strengths come from them.

And as much as I would like to say that my mother, my aunts, my cousins or I are just like my grandmother, unfortunately I can't, because after her, the mold was broken. *"Many daughters have done worthy, but she (Momma) exceeded them all."* Proverbs 31:29.

ONE MORE STEP
By Glenda Barrett

It has been several years now since I met Millie in the mountains of North Georgia. At the age of 83 she was hiking the Appalachian Trail with her son, a blind daughter and a Seeing Eye dog. After inviting them over to my house for supper, I found that Millie was a schoolteacher, and her daughter had recently lost her eyesight to diabetes.

As we shared our meal together with the dog resting at our feet, I listened as Millie talked with us about her fascinating life, and how she was planning to hike other portions of the trail. Amazed, I asked her, "How on earth do you do it?" Her answer was simple yet profound, "You know we limit ourselves as to what we can do." She continued, "When I get tired on the trail, I say to myself, 'One more step, just one more step.'" Little did I know that those words would linger with me and have a real impact on my own life.

Being inspired by this energetic woman, I also decided to broaden my own horizons. My husband and I decided to do some hiking as well. In our area there are several accesses to the Appalachian Trail that are great for short distance hiking over a few mountains so we ventured on several occasions.

One trip will always stand out in my mind. Early one summer morning we were hiking, when we rounded a curve in the trail. It was as if a spotlight had been turned on! The morning sun filtered through the trees highlighting a large hillside covered with lush, wild ferns. The scene was breathtaking! Upon hearing a trickle of water, I noticed a mountain spring surrounded by light, green moss on the bank above us. As I scooped my hands into the ice cold water to take a drink, I knew that this moment would stay with me forever.

Not only did we hike that summer, but we also went to every waterfall we could find in the area. It was not enough for me to look; I also had to know what the water felt like at the bottom of the falls. It was an exhilarating feeling to take a dip in the ice cold water after hiking several miles up a mountain. Afterwards I'd sit quietly sunning on a rock and listen to the sounds of nature around me.

It was not unusual over the years for my children and me to pack a picnic lunch and head out to a nearby park on our bicycles. Other than walking I have found there is no better view of the world than from bicycle seat. Anyway, we watched as the geese honked and flew off together landing on another part of the lake. We didn't miss the splash of a big fish either or the squirrels and rabbits scampering in the edge of the woods. On hot days we jumped in the lake and took a swim, laughing and splashing each other until we tired.

Another time we owned a boat and I decided I would learn to ski. I made several attempts but never quite got the hang of it, but I sure know what it feels like to be dragged to the bottom of the lake by the rope. Anyway, it was fun trying.

Becoming a bit more daring we decided to go on a rafting trip. As I write this I can still feel the excitement of our first trip down the Nantahala River. I can remember the coolness of the mountain air on my cheeks already moist from the dampness of the river. I felt a bit uneasy climbing into the raft, but I did not let fear stop me. Leaving the bank, we pushed off.

Having nothing to hold onto but the seat, I leaned inward as we traveled over rapids and narrowly missed rocks and logs. We all soon learned we had to do our share of rowing or we would get stranded. Before the end of the journey only one family member went overboard, and that was all in fun. There was no harm done, only a slightly scraped arm.

As I sit here writing, I can still picture the early morning sun as it filtered through the overhanging tree branches and melted the patches of fog hovering over the winding river.

As I reflect back on my life, I realize I tried several different things, maybe not always doing them well but at least trying and enjoying them. How glad I am I did. You see, at the age of 50 years old I was forced to have a spinal fusion due to two herniated disks. I healed well from the surgery, but little did I know my greatest battle was ahead of me. A few months later after complaining of numbness and pain in my legs I was diagnosed with Charcot-Marie-Tooth Disease. In a few months it was necessary to have surgery on my left foot which required me to wear a permanent brace on that foot and leg. The doctors explained to me that this was an incurable, progressive disease that would affect the hands, arms, lower legs and feet and that it was not advisable to tire the muscles. He advised me to use a scooter part of the time.

It has been seven years now since the diagnosis. At this time, I still have one brace and have had two ankle fusions on the other foot. After dealing with deep grief, I made an astonishing discovery. I learned to see this as a new beginning instead of an ending. My life became more meaningful as I learned to lean fully on my Higher Power, and I realized what was important in my life. Now I have time for hobbies I did not have time for before, such as writing and oil painting. I have time for meditation, prayer, and meaningful relationships. Many days when I go to the grocery store, someone will say, "Glenda, you are looking well." This is actually the first time in my life when I have not been running myself ragged with useless activities. For the first time in my life I am fully rested.

Looking back, I do not feel a lot of resentment because I have these limitations; you see I have already done most of the things I wanted to do in my life. Listening to folks like Millie and my own instincts, I lived my life, I wasn't just a bystander. Millie is no longer living now, but more than one time as I struggled to walk I have thought of her words, "Just one more step! We limit ourselves as to what we can do!"

I want to say to you, really live your life while you can, don't wait until you retire, or you have more money or the children are grown. Life is not predictable. You cannot know what is around the next corner. Start with small steps and create a beautiful life and live it fully and joyfully now, starting at this moment! You may find the simple life is wonderful! I did.

RECYCLING
By A. Frank Bower

Andrea takes verbal snipes at me often, poking fun at my obsessive attention to our recyclables. The cardboard, newspapers, bottles, cans and milk cartons were picked up yesterday, but I put our soda containers out this morning. She said, "It's nice that you give Gregor our stuff, but can we afford it?"

I glanced at her smirk. "Are you going to hassle me every week? Our budget isn't that tight."

"Well...it's not loose since you got laid off."

I sighed in my appreciation of her dry humor. "I was only out of work for three weeks before I got a new position."

"At about half what you made before." Andrea rolled her eyes toward the ceiling.

I grinned. "We adapted."

"I sure wanted a convertible. Fat chance now, with you giving away our nickels and dimes."

"Cute, hon. Thanks to Gregor's example, we've done fine the last two years."

Andrea laughed. "You know I'm pulling your leg. I'm glad he's your hero."

I pointed a finger into her face. "Don't forget you started it." I kissed her.

The first time I saw Gregor Drozd in 1996 I thought, *I hate bicyclists. Like there isn't enough traffic when I'm trying to get to work.* I'd finally gotten a position with a future, an income potential that could rip me out of the working class and make Andrea proud. I was new and couldn't afford to be late. A man on a bicycle was a nuisance, a speck of humanity who might do something stupid and slow my commute.

The next morning there he was peddling along Corbin Avenue, one of New Britain's longest roads. I stopped at a red light on my way to the highway entrance and noticed his bike had front and rear baskets jerry rigged of chicken wire. The front one was half full of clinking glass bottles; the back one's cans rattled. The old bicycle was a bare-bones Schwinn, no gear switchers, no frills, just a red reflector in back and a flashlight duct taped to the center of the handlebars. The traffic light changed; I sped on to my job without seeing the man.

The following day's stoplight gave me the opportunity to pay attention to the rider. He was tallish with thick, sugar-white hair topping tanned-leather skin pulled taut over skeletal features.

God, I thought, *another homeless guy. No wonder he scrounges other people's recyclables. He looks like he hasn't eaten in days.*

At dinner that evening I shook my head. Andrea asked why. I hadn't realized my response to the image of the bicycle man at our table. "I was just thinking how lucky we are. Look at this meal. It's wonderful."

"Thank you."

"You're welcome. But...I mean, here we are working our way up and the economy has so many people fighting for *any* food. It's tragic."

Andrea set her fork down.

"I saw a homeless man this morning. He looked about 70 but is probably more like 50. Just now I was picturing him here eating with us."

Andrea squinted and leaned forward. "Where did you see this man?"

"Corbin Avenue. I saw him yesterday, too."

"Was he riding a rickety old bicycle?"

"Yeah; you've seen him?"

Andrea guffawed. "Hon, he's not homeless—and he is almost 70. I thought everyone knew Gregor."

"Not me. How do *you* know him?"

"I don't. I mean, just by reputation. He's kind of a local hero."

"How so"?

"Gregor Drozd is New Britain's poster boy for the work ethic. He and his wife Irene moved here from Poland in the late seventies. Like a lot of locals, their English is broken at best, which limited the jobs they found. About three years ago they started collecting social security, but neither of them has a pension. With inflation what it is, they couldn't keep up with bills, so he came up with the idea of collecting cans and bottles to make ends meet."

"That's crazy. They're only a nickel apiece. Nobody can finance a life like that."

"Gregor does. The Drozds define frugal."

"Couldn't they get some kind of assistance... welfare or something?"

"Hon, that's the point. He's never taken a handout and never will."

"He won't be able to pedal around town forever."

Andrea smiled. "We'll see."

From that point on I paid attention to him daily, marveling at his gumption. I asked co-workers about him; most knew more than I did. I pieced together the details of his day: Out of bed at three a.m., on the road by four, first load of empties to the Central Connecticut Redemption store when it opened at seven. He received between six and eight dollars per drop off and averaged four each day, seven days a week. Everyone I talked to admired Gregor and commented that the side benefit of his hard work was that he did a lot to keep the city clean.

I watched that elderly workhorse pedal through all manner of New England weather. One day I pulled over to talk to him. I said, "Good morning."

He smiled. "Good morning. Work. Got to go."

When I got laid off in the summer of 2007, I didn't apply for unemployment benefits. Then my new work route didn't include Corbin Avenue, but I saw Gregor elsewhere. In order to cover more territory, he bought a small, gas-powered scooter and constructed a trailer from old bicycles, shopping carts and other debris he found in vacant lots and trash bins during his rounds.

I held onto Andrea this morning after our kiss. I said, "You know you keep the cans and bottles aside for me."

"Umm-hmm."

"Hon, do you remember when you first told me about him?"

"Of course."

"That day I said he wouldn't be able to pedal around town forever."

"Your point is?"

"I think I was wrong."

LETTER TO MY FIFTH GRADE TEACHER
By Michael S. Glaser

Dear Miss Lorenz:

I'm writing because I was remembering you today,
how soft and kind your voice was and how your eyes
sparkled with laughter and light

which is why I wanted to impress you
and why I was so afraid of spelling
where I knew you would discover
I was just another stupid kid.

And so, on the day of the Big Spelling Test,
I made that tiny piece of paper
and when we put our books away,
I cupped it in my hand for use
only when absolutely necessary.

And you moved up and down
the rows of our desks
pronouncing words until
you stopped next to me,
called out a word and,
when everyone was writing,
reached into my clenched fist,
took the paper and then
walked on.

You never made an example of me,
never spoke to my parents about it,
or even mentioned it to me.
And you never treated me differently either,
just went on as though nothing had happened.

But, of course, something did:
I never cheated again, Miss Lorenz.

I never stole another candy bar
or money from my mother's purse
or the top of my father's dresser.

And I am writing to thank you
for treating me with dignity
even as you caught me,
red-handed in sin.

It was as close to Grace as I have ever been.
Perhaps some day I'll know it once again.

-- Michael Glaser

IN THE MATTER OF LOVE AND REGRET
By Andrea L. Watson

The angel on earth who shared her precious life and dreams with us was adopted by our family 30 years ago. "Auntie Risa," as she came to be known, entered the world of my children as a babysitter who happened to live three blocks east of our home in Denver, Colorado. Her calling card, if she ever needed one, was that she was a 60-something woman who preferred taking care of children for long periods of time rather than three or four hours every so often. Weekends— even a month—were her forte!

Teresa arrived at our front door, gray hair flying about her, with an enormous trunk-of-a-purse packed with emergency items. Her mission was to take charge – *Of everything!* Having raised six children of her own, she knew how to charm anyone—from a wailing newborn to a ten-year-old boy convinced he was too old to need a babysitter. At the very moment she put her magical carry-all down on the single bed in our spare room, she became a member of our family, through all our joys and disappointments.

Auntie Risa knew things. *Knew things.* If a baby were fussy, she delicately placed a few droplets of warm water on its tiny feet. If a child had the chicken pox, she possessed in her portable medicine cabinet a remedy to relieve the itching. When Billie experienced a nosebleed, she could stop it on a dime by pinching the bridge of his nose, not to mention removing blood from his crib sheets with "first cold water, then hot." The day that Graham fell from a swing in our backyard and split his chin open, I came home to a butterfly bandage Teresa had contrived from scotch tape and wet toilet tissue.

And Auntie Risa was a virago if anyone attempted to frighten or cause harm to one of our children. She followed us from the tiny house on Cherry Street to what became the family home on a parkway lined with towering oak trees and elms. When we were in our new house less than two weeks, and she was watching the boys on a Tuesday morning, robbers attempted to break in with a baseball bat against our French doors. Auntie Risa ran down the narrow flight of stairs, screaming, "You won't get into our house, no siree!"

Instantly, they vanished down the alley for fear of their lives. She then proceeded to sweep up the glass and had a list of window repairmen ready on the kitchen counter when I arrived home. My son later told me he would never be afraid of robbers because "Who would ever have the guts to take on Auntie Risa?" Years later, I envisioned her following him on the airplane, in full protective gear, when he flew 2,000 miles away to attend college on the East Coast.

While my sons were busy discovering the wonders of constructing a working clock from paper, or understanding why fireflies glow in the summer night, with the help of Auntie Risa, I was learning life lessons that I hold to this day. Teresa taught me to value each of my children as an individual, for both their strengths and weaknesses; to nurture all that was best in them; and to foster the persons they might become. For her, the years of childhood were truly sacred. I always marveled at her ability to drop anything she was doing and devote herself completely to *being* with a child—building a castle from Lego's or pretending to be on a railroad train traveling to an imaginary destination, complete with passports and packed lunches. Teresa encouraged me to enjoy my children each moment, to put aside a household task or an article that had to be done, because "children grow up so very quickly—they leave us too soon." To live in that golden moment of childhood was her extraordinary gift.

Auntie Risa was a member of our family through all the years of our boys' childhood and teen-age years and all the years of my early marriage. When we were ill, she would visit us with a brand of soup known only to her: She believed that a good beef soup could cure anything, "but you have to add walnuts to it—chopped up of course—for their curative powers." I could never find a mention of that remedy in any medical text. When *she* was ill, I would visit her with some delicacy and a card made just for her by the boys, no matter how old they were.

We were friends and family through her husband's death, her own children's marriages and the births of their children. Her hosting an exchange student who never understood Auntie Risa's ministrations, probably because Teresa did not speak Japanese and the young girl only knew grammatical terms of written English such as adverbs and adjectives. We had exactly one gambling junket to Black Hawk where we both wagered $10, but not a cent more. Even the play at a theater on Colfax Avenue, where we couldn't find the tickets in her purse, so we went out for ice cream instead.

My boys grew up, outgrew Auntie Risa, although they tried to hide it, but I never stopped loving her. We had a bond of womanhood, motherhood—*relative-hood*—that transcended the role of caretaker she had begun with to the many examples of positive living she gave to me as a gift. I couldn't have survived my children's babyhood, teen-age years, leaving for college (where I cried from the airport right to her house), even the day-to-day challenges that life knew how to present. She was indomitable, unflagging, and immortal.

Or so I thought.

When I returned to teaching, and my boys were long grown, we began to lose touch. You know how that is: She was getting older. Less needed and less available. I was getting preoccupied, helping other people's children. We began the long process of growing apart although we both acknowledged it as a rite of passage.

If I have one regret in my life, a behavior I call myself to judgment on, it is that when our beloved Auntie Risa passed away of cancer, a disease she had feared all her life, I did not find the time to attend her funeral. Her children did not remember to phone me; instead, an old neighbor phoned to say the funeral was that day. I had something planned; or something that needed to be done; or the boys were long grown, and we hadn't talked in years. When I reflect on that time, all these years later, I wonder: Did I refuse to acknowledge Teresa's passing so I could pretend she was still watching over us, nurturing us, just a few steps away on Dahlia Street?

No excuse: I neglected to attend the service honoring the woman, the angel, who had been the finest jewel in our lives. No priest can absolve me of that terrible thing. No friend can tell me that Auntie Risa would have understood. Yes, I cried for her at home, all alone. My boys were told, and they wept a little over the phone. My husband held me, and we remembered her together. But there can be little forgiveness for not mourning her in public, at an altar, with the stories of our lives together told and retold. With her passing, Teresa reminded me that not only do the precious hours of childhood leave us too quickly but also the shining presence of those we love. This is the truth Teresa left for me — her finest lesson.

A SOFT PLACE TO LAND
By Abi L. Rexrode

    Sitting on Villegas' couch, I was filled with the feeling of everything being foreign and yet strangely familiar at the same time. Although I had only lived with the Villegas family for a short time, I felt as if some part of me had always known them. Margaret Villegas was busy in her kitchen down the hallway, probably fixing some Italian dish I had never heard of before. The smell of tomato sauce and oregano, although alien to me, awakened my malnourished stomach. Her husband Carlos was at the other end of the hallway working on the computer. I could hear the keyboard as he used two fingers to seek out each letter like some search and rescue mission. Aidan and Anna, their children, were across the hallway finishing their schoolwork for the day. Their bursts of laughter bounced off the walls as the light from the setting sun streamed into the living room.

    The pre-dinner atmosphere at my house had been the polar opposite. My mother would roar from the kitchen to get our butts to the dinner table. My stepfather would stagger into the kitchen, hardly making it to his seat before my mother launched into her usual squabble with him. She would grumble that he had neglected to bring in enough wood for the stove that heated our house, one of us kids had talked back to her, or her ex-husband was late with the child support again. The younger children of my family would attack the food on their plates, hoping to make a quick departure. The older ones would push their meals around with their forks, never able to find their appetites. Sometimes halfway through supper, my oldest brother would stumble into his seat with an inebriated smile. My mother's nagging forgotten for the moment; my stepfather would turn his resentment to his stepson. Using a few select insults designed to strike harder than any physical blow was capable, my stepfather would savor the instant reaction from my brother. Even when he wasn't in an intoxicated state, my brother lacked the gift of filtering his thoughts before they sped out of his mouth. After they both flung their dishes into the sink, they would storm off in separate directions. The rest of my siblings would excuse themselves, leaving my mother and me to sit alone at the table. Whenever I dared to look up from my plate, I was bewildered to see my mother silently weeping.

I had fled to college eager to escape the fights, fists, and fear that were as much a part of my house as the roof over our heads. But after failing out twice I was condemned to return to my own personal hellhole. I couldn't accept the notion of such a regression after I had held freedom in my hands for two years. With a sense of tranquility, I decided to take my own life rather than face that house again.

But it seemed that life was not quite as ready to give up on me.

Margaret and Carlos Villegas became aware of my situation through a chain of uncanny and unexplainable events. Without hesitation, they offered to help in any way they could. I was positive they were certifiably insane, but I had nothing to lose. A few months after I met them, I was in a car headed north. There is no way I could have understood the measure of their affection or how much that unconditional love would change the way I saw the world.

The Villegas' didn't just offer me a room in their house for a short while until I could make other arrangements. They welcomed me home and gave me a soft place to land after falling for so long. Instead of treating me like the new acquaintance that I was, they cared for me like a long-lost daughter. When I expected yelling and mistreatment, I was blessed with words of encouragement and open arms. Before I moved in with them, I had only seen brief glimpses of optimism in a world filled with hurting and hatred. Now I had my own personal guards ready to comfort and protect me. I was a dried-out sponge plunging to an infinite fountain of warm, refreshing water.

As much as I enjoyed the endless flood of love, I was afraid that it would soon come to a halt. Surely the Villegas' would realize how unworthy, dim-witted, and hideous I was. There had to be some trick, some catch, something I was missing in the equation. Although I needed so much to believe that I was finally secure and that life could be worth living, I had too much conflicting experience to expect anything so positive.

"I don't deserve you," I told Margaret one day, needing to comprehend how she could care for me so passionately. "I'll never be able to repay you for rescuing me. I just don't understand."

"That's the beauty of love, babe," she replied.

I lived with the Villegas' for almost four years. During that time they sheltered me, helped me deal with my past, and even visited me at the hospital when I was on suicide watch. They showered me with Christmas and birthday presents, supported me when I went back to college, and always made sure I had enough to eat. But more than the warm blankets on winter nights and vacations to the beach, I am eternally grateful for the love that they surrounded me with. I'm indebted for all the hugs that held me when I was crying, the late-night conversations when I was afraid to sleep, and the brilliant sparkle in their eyes when they looked at me. The Villegas' reminded me how to laugh. They believed in me, even when I couldn't. They taught me what it really meant to love and be loved.

Although I have an apartment of my own and can afford to buy my own food and clothing, I know that the Villegas' are still there whenever I may need them. They are more than just good friends. They are my coaches, my parents, and my guardian angels in the flesh. Most of the time, it's hard for me to believe that just a short time ago I was ready to give up.

When I look back at those first few weeks of living with the Villegas family I can't help but remember how even though I had no idea what I had gotten myself into, I was overwhelmed with a sense of security. Sitting on their couch, it was like some essential part of me knew that I was finally where I belonged.

BRICK
By Bridges DelPonte

A black-and-white photocopy of a brick. Or actually a photocopy of a brick rubbing. My sister, Dolores, sent it to me after I moved from Boston to Florida to teach and to warm my middle-aged bones. I keep it tacked to my office corkboard and it still can make me tear up. Not that I normally get emotional about building materials. But this brick is something special. A simple block installed in the brick path to the newly-renovated Canton Public Library, a 1902 columned architectural gem, with an enormous leaded glass dome above the circulation desk. Dolores and her husband bought the brick to honor our father and help defray the costs of library modernization. You don't get much space on a brick so you better make it good. "Joseph Ponte. Do It Now."

For a man who loved to poke fun at the high and mighty, he would relish the idea of the whole town walking all over him every single day. But then the public library was his kind of place, a temple of learning for regular folk, including a man who suffered infantile paralysis as a boy, spoke only Portuguese until grade school, and cut short his college studies on the GI bill to support his growing family. Machinist Mate II, Navy, Korea. Always happy to pick up a military man thumbing his way home, sliding open the heavy door of the high cab of his Wonder Bread truck or squishing him into our cramped station wagon as we headed to the Cape for a long day trip, listening to American Top 40. He loved being buried in the hot sand, a balmy place to rest his weary muscles before he drove our boisterous tribe back home that same day.

In his brief respites between juggling one full-time job and a slew of part-time ones, he devoured books in a small upholstered living room chair with a wobbly three-way metal lamp hanging above it. As a speed reader, he rapidly paged through hefty volumes with his bifocal glasses resting on the tip of his nose. An aromatic curl of smoke rose from a curved pipe between his full lips and teeth, smoldering with Half and Half or Sir Walter Raleigh tobacco, or the occasional Garcia y Vega cigar.

"I don't inhale, but since I smoke I can't tell you not to," he told us, knowing that stealing the rebellion out of it would yield nine nonsmokers. Probably applying some scrap of reverse psychology he discovered in a book.

The few books we owned, a red leather Bible, the prized set of Funk and Wagnall encyclopedias and hard cover Reader's Digest compilations of the classics, were carefully preserved behind the glass hutch doors of a drop-front secretary desk in the crowded passageway at the foot of the stairs. A skeleton key poked out of the desk's lock. But we all had blue paper library cards with rectangular numbered metal stamp plates for checking out books, a regular part of our week along with Catholic mass where he often read to the congregation as a lector. My parents made sure we read plenty of books and got them back to the library promptly. At two cents a day, they had no extra money and little patience for late book fines.

"Do it now," he said. His mantra for everything from returning library books to pursuing one's life goals. He believed life was short so get on with it before it evaporates.

At dinner, we sat on battered wooden chairs and a long side bench around a long plywood board covered with a red-and-white plastic tablecloth. We bounced around arguments about that day's current events from the newspaper. The Vietnam War. School busing. Race discrimination. Married priests. Union corruption. Watergate politics. Gun control. The contrarian in him reveled in playing the devil's advocate, weaving words into provocative assertions that opposed his own personal views. He liked to waggle his index finger, permanently crooked from an infection, in the air or pound the kitchen table to punctuate a key argument. And for dessert, we traded rapid-fire puns, jokes, and wisecracks; a chorus of little brown-faced Ali, floating like butterflies, stinging like bees, with words not fists.

Those dinner debates were good practice for his subsequent service as shop steward, disputing work rules with management or fighting to integrate the local Teamsters union. One time, he traveled to NAACP headquarters to help a black driver, named Bobby, who got fired after white co-workers rained down the "N" word and threatened him until he pulled out a knife. At his grievance hearing, Dad argued and argued until he wore both sides out with his volley of declarations and comebacks until Bobby got his job back. They were no real match for someone who fended off nine rambunctious kids in verbal jousts every night. Float like a butterfly, sting like a bee.

Despite his love of words, it drove him crazy to lose regularly at Scrabble to my mother or to one of us. He once flipped over a wooden "Q" pretending it was a blank tile in an effort to win one close match. But he had to confess immediately since he found no joy in cheating at words or anything else. Unfortunately, he couldn't cheat years of arthritis pain from an old Navy injury exacerbated by decades of jumping on and off trucks and lifting heavy bread racks. Or a failing heart weary from working incredibly long hours and smoking his beloved pipes and cigars. Or taking too hard the sibling squabbles and troubles that bedeviled any family. After all that reading and all those words, he slipped away unexpectedly in his sleep one April night in 1985, without whispering a single syllable.

Before he passed, I knew he never fully understood my drive to become an attorney. He puzzled over my lugging those heavy books, pouring over lengthy court cases, pushing myself to achieve while juggling part-time work and law school. He never intended our family's daily mental gymnastics to somersault into the rough and tumble of legal practice. My Dad expected me to settle down and raise a family, arguing with a passel of children around a kitchen table rather than with other lawyers around a conference room table. My Dad stood too close to it to see that I had woven together so much of him into my own path, creating something new and totally different from his host of life lessons.

He would have been thrilled to see me become a law school professor, for he held all teachers in high esteem. All those books, all those words, all that learning. I often think of him when I stand in front of my class of eager law students. We discuss and debate complex legal issues in our interactive classroom filled with all of the latest technological wizardry. Echoes of those nights around our modest kitchen table contesting everything under the sun are never far away. Every semester, I try to coax them to read more, to study harder, to dream bigger, and to stop procrastinating in their studies, and in their lives. Read that case, call that friend, shoot for that internship, finish that assignment, fix that resume, improve that argument, and go thank that parent. "Do it now."

MATRON SAINT OF THE THROW AWAY
By Claudia B. Van Gerven

I fold the Hallmark sack carefully, slide it gently
onto the shelf. My husband sees
my hoarding, as a sort of stinginess that denies
the endlessness of commerce, the resourcefulness of trees,
an insult to his largesse. He shakes his head perplexed
at my horde of the trivial.

My grandmother washed paper plates, used them again,
cut up junk mail for note paper, her dresser drawers crammed
with old chocolate boxes full of lost
buttons. She never threw away a birthday card
 -- all the best wishes of friends and children, the twenty-three
grandchildren,
tied with odd bits of string. Not a tablespoon
of peas nor a word slipped past her regard.

She taught me the decency of things--
how a broken dish could decorate a garden or a torn dress
could fill with summer breezes as kitchen curtains.

When I cut my hoarded sack open, I will savor
the feel of good paper, smooth it tenderly
into gift wrap, carefully tape the folded ends, retie
the mauve ribbon from a bag of bath salts I soaked in
offer these small shape-shiftings, these tiny resurrections
to a disposable world.

INSPIRATION
By Cynthia Hollamon-Cook

It was an average Monday for me at my place of employment. At best it was hectic, draining and challenging on many levels, as working with elderly people with memory issues often can be. Plodding through my day, trying hard to put on that "Disneyland" smile our administrator so often encourages us to have was challenging enough, but throwing in a two-hour staff meeting in the middle of it sent my anxiety to its maximum level.

For four years, I have been trying to talk myself into "having compassion." What seems, by my observation, to come so naturally to my coworkers proves to be a daily challenge for me. Not to say it is not challenging for them. They face the same stressors that I do everyday, but they seem to handle them differently. This is not my calling. I know this like I know when my children don't feel well, just by looking in their eyes. I know this like I know my family loves me, without them ever having to say a word.

Aside from the meeting, this was a typical Monday. I rushed through my tasks so as to go to the meeting, not mindful at all of the moment I was in. Instead, my mind was racing with thoughts. Did I remember to take out the trash? Did I remind this resident to take a shower? Did I give that resident their protein shake? What will I make for dinner when I get home? Will I ever *get* home?

We sat at our familiar places in the meeting room with the agenda in front of us. We prepared to go over everything that had been gone over and over again. But this was a special day because in walked a very special person. A man we had known, until very recently, as our nurse. I had heard prior to the meeting that he may come to say goodbye. Due to a serious illness, his doctor advised him to take early retirement, immediately. It was a shock to us. Walking by his empty office and no longer seeing his beautiful photography he displayed for so long made me feel a void in the last few days.

As I sat, I thought about how much I missed this person that I really didn't even know. I knew his smile and his kind voice and that his gentleness with our residents meant something. I knew that when I saw him in his office, with paperwork up to his ears, that he was busier then I could ever even imagine. I knew that he was there, but I never really saw him.

Feeling a bit sad at this revelation, but still happy he was at our meeting, I listened as he began to speak. I was not prepared. He began by telling us a little about his situation. He then told us he loved each and every one of us and I knew that he meant it. He explained that we all have a unique gift and that we need to realize our working relationships with each other extend way beyond this time and place and will be remembered for years to come. We touch each other in some way. We affect each other more then we realize. And as he was saying these words, his voice broke as he tried to suppress his emotions.

As he continued, my eyes filled with tears and my heart ached. A lump reached my throat just as sudden shame washed over me for all of the times I have complained. For all of the times I have taken for granted the gifts in my life. And I realized too that I was grieving the loss of this man, even though he was not gone, he wasn't with us anymore in the way that we knew him. The way that felt safe in our perfect, yet sometimes imperfect little world at work.

I have heard words like these before, but I haven't listened. His sincerity begged me to on this day. I listened. The days I so often rush through. The people I don't think I affect, and the time that I have left on this earth, begged me to. I have a lot to learn, but I am teachable. Our former nurse and our friend taught me by his example of kindness, his simple yet profound words. So many times he went unnoticed as I hurried past him, trying to get through my day. It begs the question, what else have I been missing? What beauty and inspiration am I passing up as my mind races to the future instead of where I am, at this moment?

At the end of his talk, he pulled out a flute and began to play the most beautiful music. It was such a perfect ending to this bittersweet moment. We all clapped and smiled and heaviness could be felt throughout the room as he said goodbye. We told him to come back and visit. I smiled at the thought but yet I knew somehow that I would never see him again. I guess as time goes on, so do people.

Since this meeting I realize now that although my work may not be my calling, it is where I am at this time. And what *about* compassion? I think that it is extremely hard to be compassionate towards other people if you don't have any for yourself. I think that's where I will start; with myself. Thank you to our friend and former nurse whose inspiring words and kindness let me know I matter at work and in this world.

A TASTE OF UNCONDITIONAL LOVE
By Elaine Morgan

When I was a child, I thought Grandma was only about my stomach. Every Sunday morning, hand-forged pasta dried on white cotton bed sheets. Water rattled in a large aluminum pot. Wafts of garlic, tomatoes and basil circulated on the blades of an old electric table-top fan.

Grandma prepared "made from scratch" meals under the direction of Italian opera which floated through the corded front of the cathedral-shaped radio sitting on a table in the parlor. She was an Italian High Priestess in a well-worn cotton house dress which bloomed perennial faded blue flowers. She labored within the confines of the sacred grove of her own home, celebrating a daily ceremony in the preparation of food for her family in the sanctuary of her own kitchen. At the time, I thought this was what love was all about.

As the first grandchild to be born into the family, I had no competition for many years. What I had was Grandma's undivided attention. She also had mine. She always threw her head back and laughed heartily when I missed a stitch or discovered that the bread dough I made did not rise as it should.

On occasion, in the middle of a crocheting lesson or a dissertation on the preparation of pasta sauce, Grandma would suddenly pause and look deeply into my eyes. Then she would smile broadly and the walnut lines on her face would soften. During those precious moments, she repeated the same affirmation: *Elena, always remember what I tell you now. Whether you are wrong or you are right, you will always be right in your Grandma's eyes.*

At the time, I did not realize that I was being mentored as well as showered with a love which had no strings attached to it. I only knew that what she said felt good and that no one else told me they would continue to love and approve of me even if I did something wrong or made a mistake.

After her death, the essence of her affirmation remained with me like strange, ancient hieroglyphs which had been carved on the Rosetta stone of my own heart.

Somewhere between young adulthood and middle age, her simple words also made a transition from a bud to a blossoming flower. I realized that Grandma had given me permission to be human. In her wisdom and life experience, she had chosen not to burden her first grandchild with expectations of perfection. In her own simple way, she was letting me know it was alright for me to make wrong choices. She was forgiving me in advance of my foolishness and folly on the journey of life. She was also supporting my moments of wisdom as well. Grandma was teaching me to love myself unconditionally, to honor myself for doing what I thought was right, and to forgive myself for the times I went astray.

Today, I realize Grandma wasn't all about my stomach. She was also about my head and my heart, how I thought about myself and how I felt about myself as I responded to life's conflicting and paradoxical experiences.

She taught me how to sew and how to cook, but she also taught me about self-acceptance and self-love through her generous example. Her gift to me was the lasting gift of emotional well-being. It was her positive response to who I was and how she felt about me which has been my guide throughout my life.

Over the years, I have often opened this gift on many occasions. I often think about Grandma when I laugh at my own foibles and I can almost hear that sweet voice speaking in broken English telling me one more time... *You'll always be right in your Grandma's eyes.*

WITCH OR ANGEL
By Eric G. Müller

At the time I didn't think much of the short and odd meeting, but over the years I've thought back on it again and again, mostly while feeling down, or going through a hard time. I have often wondered at its significance.

My walk back home from my temporary job at a chocolate warehouse took me through the woods. Not just any woods, but the Black Forest in southern Germany where I lived for two years. Mostly I was alone for that last stretch, though on occasion I'd spot some lovers or a tramp. One warm, autumn afternoon, just before sundown – it was later than usual, because I'd worked overtime – I saw an old, bent over little crone, wading through the thick undergrowth, at quite some distance off the narrow path. A big wicker basket hung from the crook of her arm and her head was covered with a threadbare, dark blue shawl, sprinkled evenly with small white dots. Leaves, grass and dirt stuck to her black coat and grimy-grey apron she wore underneath. I stopped and watched how she slowly parted the branches and ferns, peering and feeling her way through the underbrush. Intermittently she'd pluck at something and put it into her basket, mumbling. She looked like she'd stepped right out of a Grimm's fairy tale.

"What are you doing?" I asked curiously. She stopped, surprised at the intrusion. Her muttering ceased, though her jaw still moved slightly and she tried to stand upright, which still left her looking bent and frail. Her wizened face was unwashed and weather-beaten. I stepped off the path to join her. She watched me approach with her opaque, watery, light blue eyes, tucked into crumpled skin. Her face was questioning, and it dawned on me she might be afraid. "What are you looking for?" I asked as pleasantly as I could to put her at ease.

She hesitated, then grabbed awkwardly for something in her basket with her right hand and said, "Here." Her tiny, gnarled fingers exposed three fresh raspberries. It crossed my mind how dirty her hand must be, but I accepted the red fruit anyway.

They tasted exceptionally good. "You're collecting raspberries?"

Again she hesitated and looked straight at me. Though her eyes were filmy they were awake and penetrating. At last, as if she'd satisfied her scrutiny, she broke off and spoke, "Yes, and I also look for blackberries, mushrooms, herbs and roots." By the way she coughed and cleared her throat of excess phlegm I could tell she was unaccustomed to speaking much. "This forest still has a lot to give, if you take the time." Her voice was as feeble as her thin, bent body. Her gaunt face quivered with every word.

"What do you mean – still?"

"Nowadays, many of the herbs are harder to find. They don't grow as they used to." She paused and cleared her throat and chest again. "Even the raspberries are getting less," and she smiled, revealing worn gums, studded with yellowed stumps. "Here have some more." She fumbled in her rattan basket, and offered me another handful with her cracked and shaky fingers."

"So, you know a lot about plants?" I asked, popping two more raspberries into my mouth, no longer caring about her dirty fingers. The hag intrigued me. I wondered where she lived, how she lived, with whom she lived, and what she knew. I liked the idea of meeting a real live witch in the Black Forest. Could she cast spells?

"Oh yes, since I've been a little girl," she began. "My mother used to sell herbs to people in the towns and villages around here. That was when the doctors and pharmacists still used what we collected." I noticed that her voice was no longer quite as cracked and slow. "I always helped her, and she taught and showed me what to look for... but that was long ago." She cleared her throat again and chuckled. "Now I just gather them for myself... and for the animals."

The sun had set and it was getting dark. We continued talking. By now I was sure that she'd not spoken to anyone for quite a while, maybe months, or even years. And after she'd cleared her throat a few more times, she spoke with greater fluency and an almost youthful flair. To my surprise, she was the one now asking the questions: "What makes a young man like you want to talk to an old woman who is gathering berries and herbs in a forest? Where do you come from? Where are your parents? Do you have any brothers or sisters?" In the beginning I answered them cordially and briefly, but she kept on probing deeper, wanting to know more – what I wanted to do with my life, what hopes and visions I had for the future, my fears, issues and problems... on and on. Each question led to another, more intimate one. Though I tried to veer the conversation back to her life, I never succeeded.

We talked and talked while it got darker and darker. I could hardly see her anymore, save for her eyes – no longer filmy, but clear and glistening. And in the end, not even those, just our disembodied voices hovering back and forth in the hushed forest that now was utterly black – true to its name. Here we were, the two of us: an old woman and a young man in the dark thickets, away from the path, midst mushrooms, ferns and thistles; two strangers talking with uncanny familiarity. She was a shadow, a phantom, a specter, and I was opening and answering to it. Her questions were now coming in fast succession, and there was no more clearing of the throat, nor any hesitation. I told her about my life in South Africa, how I'd left the country for political reasons; my time in Switzerland, jobbing and traveling around; my move to Germany to play in a band; my musical ambitions; my failures; my studies; my dream of living in America; my family; my struggles to come to terms with spirituality. I told her things that I'd kept pent up within myself for years; secrets I hardly dared to confront, even to myself; wounds I'd ignored; guilt I'd denied; the lack of compassion that had hardened me; love that I so desperately yearned for. My words were like tears that had finally found their release.

At last, as we both paused and found our breath, she felt for my hands in the darkness, gripped them forcefully with surprisingly strong fingers, and thanked me for taking the time to talk to an old, lonely woman. With that she merged and disappeared into the dense, black night and was gone. I felt strangely elated.

Now I understand why that nocturnal meeting, over which I've pondered for so many years, was so significant. What she did – this good and aged witch, this weird and wise fey – was to talk to me at a time when there was nobody in the world with whom I could talk, really talk; when there was nobody in the world who would listen, really listen, when there was nobody at all who took an interest in me. Now, on looking back, I can recognize that the memory of our meeting always surfaced when I was caught in a time of need, facing a crisis, dealing with depression or other difficulties of one kind or another. The memory inevitably gave me strength, as if she herself was coming once again to help me out. In turn, it has given me the strength to help others – being there for people in need as she'd once been there for me. Now I know that when I met her in the woods, so long ago, I was blessed. Yes, that's it – blessed by an angel.

A VOICE FROM THE PAST
By Elayne Clift

Not long ago I received a letter from my favorite seventh grade teacher. Up in years now, she is a woman who made an enormous difference in my life, sustaining me at a time when adolescents can believe that life is asking too much of them. Hearing from her all these years later is a great gift.

"I am looking at a beautiful picture of you that you gave me in 1958," she wrote. "Where have the years gone since I was your teacher?"

She had found me through the people who bought our house after my father went bankrupt in the 1960s. They knew of my whereabouts because of publicity for a book I'd published. "Your house was sold to our oldest and dearest friends," she said. "When I was growing up I played in the field where your old home now stands."

She must have told me that on one of the afternoons when I visited her after school but if she did, I don't recall it. I do remember how much I loved sitting with her in the solitude of that empty classroom. I can see her now, sitting behind her desk, her large, graceful body leaning forward in a starched white blouse, hands crossed in front of her. She smiles, waiting for me to speak. And slowly I do. I talk about my mother's illness, my father's business losses, my older sister and younger brother — all of them gone now.

I probably don't speak of my new, terrifying inability to recite in class; that horror is too upsetting. But she knows, of course; that's why she never calls on me to speak aloud for more than a moment. She knows, too, that I am being ostracized by my classmates. Other students are cruel when they don't understand absent mothers, frightened fathers and a child's responsibility.

I spent the entire year enveloping myself in the warmth of our after-school conversations until I didn't need to anymore because I had recovered myself. Then one day she told me a secret: "I'm going to have a baby," she said. I was glad but also sad, because I knew she wouldn't be at school the next year.

"My husband and I have a daughter, whom I believe you came to see," she wrote in her letter to me. Yes, I went to visit when her daughter was a year old, and I remember how softly her mother loved her.

My teacher wrote to me because she had learned of the memoir

I'd written to honor my lost family. "I have often wondered how life treated you," she said. So I phoned her when the letter arrived to tell her that life had treated me well. I was a teacher myself now, I shared, and a writer, married with two children.

"I taught for 33 years and have missed it greatly," she told me. "Now I'm a voice from the past to say I have thought of you often over the decades."

And I have thought of her – dear Shirley Myers -- for she is among a handful of people whom I remember with a grateful heart for helping me through those difficult days of my growing up when life seemed bleak. Her kindness and gentle demeanor were beacons of light guiding me into maturity.

It gives me great joy to say that some of my students have said I've helped ease them forward on their own journeys. As a teacher, I could wish for nothing more, because there can be no greater gift than being a person who makes a difference in someone else's life. It makes me proud to follow in the footsteps of someone whose affection and attention pushed me onward and pulled me through.

WHEREVER YOU GO, THERE YOU ARE
By Janet Tamez

The end of the school year was approaching and summer was well on its way. It was my first year as a middle school teacher and I really didn't know how I made it. Revisiting middle school was hard; I had forgotten how cruel children were at that age, and yet how sensitive and insecure. Bullying wasn't just for the students. On Monday, you could be the target of their antics. The entire class would be laughing at you because Monica secretly called you a witch in 'code talk.' But by Tuesday she'd come slithering through your door late in the afternoon while her friends weren't around to apologize.

This wasn't something I was used to. During my school days I was a popular cheerleader and liked by everyone. Now, I was the evil teacher kids wrote about on the bathroom stalls. My rookie dreams of making a difference, of nurturing the future generation were shattered. It was a tough year; only 23, I still felt much like a child myself. I didn't know how to deal with ungrateful, disrespectful middle-schoolers. Quite frankly, I'd often felt compelled to write back, *"You ain't seen nothing yet!"* on the bathroom stalls under "Ms. Tamez is a -- " It wasn't until later that I realized the magical way children make you grow up. The whole time they were a pack of hounds sniffing out my weaknesses and testing every inch of my patience. Things were so bad, that I chose not to return the following school year. Instead, I decided, I would go on a spiritual retreat and find my true calling.

I turned to the only person who I knew could help me, my yoga instructor. She gave me a website with a directory of spiritual retreats. So, it wasn't surprising that when I came across a "Jungle Goddess Retreat," I booked it right away. Slipping away into the Belizean jungle, finding my inner Goddess, embarking on a spiritual journey with like-minded women, was exactly what I needed. However, things didn't turn out as planned. A devastating hurricane hit Belize a week before the trip. Rivers flooded, roads were closed, and food was scarce. Jen, the spiritual guide, called to inform me that the trip had been cancelled. I was heartbroken. I needed this magical and mystical trip. It was the only hope I had to finding myself. Jen sensed the disappointment in my voice and mentioned that although the retreat was canceled, she would be traveling to Belize in search of property. I could go with her, she said, as a travel companion. The trip would cost a bit more since I wouldn't be splitting the costs with other women. Although the roads were closed, I would still have a chance to see some Mayan ruins and lodge in the jungle. Yes! I agreed. Whatever, the cost, whatever the circumstance, I knew I had to go to Belize. I knew if I made to the top of a Mayan pyramid, all my questions would be answered.

The day finally arrived and I met Jen at the airport. Expecting to find a peaceful spiritual teacher whose presence would uplift my soul, instead I encountered an impatient, temperamental mother and her helpless child. I was in awe as I witnessed Jen flare her nostrils, snap at the car rental attendant during a mix up, then bolt out the office, pull out a cigarette, and smoke it nervously as she twitched her head back and forth. "My brother you're f*ing up!" she shouted in an annoyed yet philanthropic sort of way. I couldn't believe my eyes. "How could a spiritual leader smoke?" I thought. "Isn't she supposed to handle life's obstacles with ease and grace rather than a temper tantrum? Did I just hear vulgar street language?" Once again my dreams were crushed. I had put all my hope into Jen. She was supposed to give me insight; was supposed to be my wise crone, my Mr. Miyagi.

Unfortunately, the trip continued on the same note it started with. Jen never caught a break; from flat tires to stolen purses to losing her passport. I guess you could blame her wild ways or curse the fiery planets that ruled her but the late night partying, drinking, and hanging out with the wrong crowd did not help at all. It was sad to see her daughter suffer from embarrassment as her mother flirted with and kissed strange men; sad to see a little girl become the adult while her mother pranced around like a careless teenager. I couldn't believe how a lost soul could parade herself as spiritual leader. A wise friend once told me, "You teach what you need to learn most." And I guess this was the case; Jen needed to find herself as much as I did.

I came home from Belize a wiser woman. Climbing the top of Xunantunich during the summer solstice on a full moon didn't give me the epiphany I needed. Feeling the ancient limestone in my fingertips was moving; gazing down with a bird's eye view at the luscious tree tops was exhilarating. Life changing? No.

Ironically, I learned from Jen after all. The lesson wasn't as beautiful as I had painted it. Sometimes the answers don't come to you on top of a mountain like they did for Moses. This time they came from chaos. I thought back to the many ways Jen's daughter needed her. The nights I babysat while her mother partied late in the evening and slept in on her morning hangovers. I realized that in chaos, children may act like adults and adults may act like children; that the word "teacher" doesn't make you one; even if you are crazy enough to lead 20 disillusioned women into the Belizean jungle. That in any moment a teacher can be the student, and a student the teacher.

Order was necessary. There's something quite scary in children who grow up too fast. I thought back to my classroom and realized I shouldn't have expected my students to behave like adults; I should have been the adult. The truth is there are too many children in the world and not enough adults to guide them. In fact, it wasn't unusual that I later learned why I was lead to Belize. Belize is a 'child' country where almost half its population is children under the age of 15. The message was clear; it was time for me to grow up. So the following school year I returned, this time as a *teacher* willing and ready to guide my students, to accept them for all that they are: *children*.

LIFE LESSON:
LIGHTING THE INTERNAL SPARK OF HOPE
By Karen R. Elvin

I have come to believe that inside every human being, no matter how disabled, injured or ill, there exists a soul waiting to be touched by the arts, Christ's love and friendship. A close friend who suffered with Parkinson's once shared with me that we need friends during our illnesses. We are never intended to be alone. That was never more evident to me as when I met Arnold.

I was in the middle of my career as a traveling home therapist, when Arnold came into my life. He was bedridden, deeply depressed, wearing pajamas and living in a small dark room in a home care center. A church friend shared with me that Arnold's stroke had left him with limited right side body mobility, aphasic, and suffering from frequent migraines and dizzy spells. No one knew how to minister to, reach out to, or bring light into Arnold's world. . If anyone needed a friend, it was Arnold.

Could my friendship and my training in art therapy be able to stimulate Arnold's communication? It is known that significant connection between our brain cells are developed through art, music, writing and body movement. Art therapy holds so much hidden potential for patients of stroke, dementia, Alzheimer's, and more. At one time, in Arnold's youth, he had been known to paint. I was optimistic I could help him ... and so our journey in friendship began.

I initiated a multi-sensory approach in weekly visits; bringing objects from the natural world to Arnold's bedside. The first week, I placed a shell in his hand and led him in guided imagery and reflection. I offered herbal lotions to his immobile, rigid hands. A thriving green plant was placed upon his window sill, and opening the room curtains, I invited healing rays of sunshine back into Arnold's life. Together we spent time listening to endless tapes of the sounds of nature and ocean waves. Each week, before leaving, I also offered a brief prayer for healing. It was my intent that Arnold's body and soul could be touched and led into a healing state. The outcome of healing, I left to God.

Over weeks, Arnold and I viewed countless colored photos on calendars, magazines, cards, and in books of sailing boat scenes. Arnold began to draw and paint his favorite objects. Soon, I placed a pillow, pad of paper and soft drawing charcoal in his hand. Together, hand on hand, we drew lines, suggestive of water, boats, the beach, shells, and more. After three months, his church friends purchased Arnold a box of watercolors and brushes. They hoped it may motivate Arnold to continue to paint and live again.

One day as we were searching the photos for ideas, Arnold became very excited and his eyes lit up. He gestured to a photo of a lighthouse. I set up a small table and chair near Arnold's bedside and introduced Arnold to try his left, non-dominant hand in painting. Life was challenging for Arnold and his terrible migraine headaches often came on suddenly; causing him to shut down and stop painting. Teaching him relaxation exercises and to breathe deeply as they came on began to help him to resume painting often after ten minutes.

At first, Arnold's pictures were small and half finished, until one particular week when he indicated he wished to paint a new lighthouse. This time the paper was longer, and Arnold was sitting taller. This lighthouse turned into the "Red and White Lighthouse." In this art piece, he painted a bright yellow beam against the dark brown sky and cliffs. This picture was Arnold's turning point: the spark of hope for renewal we had patiently awaited. More pictures followed.

Towards the end of our art sessions together, Arnold's church friends wished to sponsor a small art exhibit of Arnold's paintings . . . testimony to his resiliency, road of recovery from stroke and depression, and his amazing story of new life via art therapy: his bright yellow beam of hope signaling to all and demanding of an audience to look and listen.

For me, I learned a life lesson; that there is no hopeless situation. Love demands patience, trial, and prayer, but most of all a call or spark of the Infinite Creator. As a lighthouse beacons to the sailing ship, a glimmer of light and hope was reignited in Arnold and those who cared about him, burning even more brightly than before. As in Arnold's lighthouse, I know in every human being there holds a universal spark of hope.

MATRIARCH
By Bob Moreland

Beatrice Cortéz Threadgill Law
a name in elegance o'ershadowed
only by the woman herself;
who, in her twenties
attended women's college
with a voracious appetite for the word.

Cultured, groomed and refined,
broke Southern tradition to marry
a dashing adventurer;
who persistently wooed her
throughout that long summer,
until her definite no became "Yes".

She bore him four children
during the early Depression.
Marjorie Jane died-
survived by two brothers;
my mother, who, instilled with empathy
brought me to see her.

The opulence of high summer
her gardens in bloom
as we walk
amidst cannas and ribbon cane.
Lessons taught, both gentle and hard;
she read to me her treasures.

Later, cataracts clouded her eyes,
blindness stole the words.
I read to her
and hoped and prayed that her
time was not so short-
that she didn't have to go.
When at last she passed on
my mother forbade me see

so I would
remember the elegant matriarch
whom I cherished.
It was as if she never died.

How I long to go back in time
embrace her small frame
and hear her say,
"I am so proud of you-
you did what I taught.
Now go and teach your very own."

                              Previously published in *Eternal Not Immortal*

WHEN SILENCE SPEAKS
By Kathleen Gerard

"Well, you certainly breathe new life into the adage, '*It's the quiet ones you've got to watch out for,*'" my Women's Studies professor began at our one-on-one conference near the end of the term. She slipped on her reading glasses and opened a file labeled with my name. While she thumbed through the pages of one of my essays, I nervously started to pick at my cuticles. "Quite frankly, I'm surprised you had all this in you," she said. "You've barely spoken a word all semester."

"It's - It's a big group," I stuttered, knowing full-well that the class had a very small enrollment for a state college—20 students. It was held in a lounge with sofas and end tables. We drank coffee. The unstructured setting was designed to affect a relaxed atmosphere that encouraged informal group discussion and the offering up of opinions. But my cautious, shy, grossly-inhibited voice was easily obscured by much more expressively confident, freewheeling students. "Conversation's not my forte," I said in my defense.

"Granted," the professor agreed. "But class participation is 50 percent of your grade."

I felt my face flush hot and my throat, parch. When I looked down, my cuticles were now bleeding. I was well aware of what was coming next, as I'd had similar conversations with teachers since elementary school.

"You're averaging an A on your papers and tests, but you're failing class participation." The teacher gazed at me over her bifocals. "How do you feel about my giving you a C as your final grade?"

My stomach dropped. "I'm not a C student." The thought of getting anything less than an A grade was crushing. "I know I'm not very vocal, but I wish you'd reconsider. You can see from my papers, the effort I put in. I did the best I could with participation. Really, I did."

Both of my parents were educators, and they'd raised me and my siblings always encouraging—and expecting—that we'd do and be our best, in and out of the classroom. At times like these, when my best didn't measure up with success, there was nothing harder—or more frustrating.

"It says here that you're a Communications major," the professor said, peering into my file again.

"Yes. I'm majoring in Photography - Photojournalism, actually."

"Ah-ha, the quintessential observer," she said. "But I figured with your demeanor and how well you express your ideas on paper, you were more a lover of words than pictures."

Her perception planted a seed within me. Photography was all I ever wanted since I was kid. But soon after I'd started the college program, I questioned if I really had the right personality to become a photojournalist. I learned that one needed a passion for being with people, coupled with a sense of spontaneity. My timid, methodical nature often worked against me as capturing the real world on film was a far cry from shooting photos for the high school newspaper and yearbook. My idealized enthusiasm began to fade.

I had always been better at reading books and writing essays than taking tests, and I'd always kept a journal — it was the perfect way for a shy introvert to articulate all her feelings. But I'd never thought seriously about writing — not until that day.

"I'll make a deal with you about your grade," the professor said, flipping my file closed and peeling off her glasses. "The essay you wrote about your parents' marriage was riveting. How about you deliver it at the literature festival, and we'll consider it extra credit toward that participation grade of yours?"

Sweat broke out on the palms of my hands at the thought of standing before an auditorium full of people, yet keeping my perfect grade-point-average meant everything to me. Therefore, I took a breath deep enough to plunge into an oceanic abyss and extended my hand. The professor quickly firmed her fingers around mine. *Done.* She sealed the deal before I could give it another thought.

I laid awake nights afterward, and for days on end, I practiced reading the essay aloud to commit it to memory. But on the evening of the event, with my knees knocking behind the podium, I gazed out at the rows upon rows of faces, and my mind suddenly went blank. I broke into a cold, clammy sweat, where it seemed that my entire grasp of the English language oozed from my pores along with waves of perspiration. *I'm gonna be sick. I'm gonna regurgitate the slice of pizza I had for dinner - right here in front of hundreds of people.* I shivered at the thought of tomato sauce spewing over the black marks on the paper and strings of mozzarella cheese dangling from the microphone. *How gross! How humiliating! What was I thinking? Why didn't I just have a piece of toast for dinner? And why couldn't I just be satisfied with a C grade for once in my life?* But in the midst of this mental diatribe, something within me urged that I just stare down at the words on the pages that were trembling in my hands and start reading. My voice quivered weakly as I began. Then I cleared my throat and pressed on, growing more confident, sentence by sentence. I read the story of my parents' marriage. I'd written it as if it were a fairytale until the story finally climaxed with my father's sudden death 20 years into their marriage when I was just 14 years old.

By the time I uttered the last word of the story, I was met with a stunning silence that made my heart beat in my throat. *Oh my goodness! They hated it. Barfing would've been far more memorable!* Yet, when I looked up and gazed at the tender expressions staring back at me—including that of my professor, who was moved to tears and who rose to her feet, clapping—I was met with a shower of applause. At the reception afterward, I was amazed to learn how my words had touched people on a personal level. They had not only roused the hearts and minds of many people in the auditorium, but they had stirred something deep within me, too.

"How does it feel to be an A student?" the professor asked, giving me a pat on the back after the reading.

"What a relief!" I sighed.

There was pride beaming in her gaze when she said, "Then I guess all is right with the world again."

But the world for me was never the same. And it was all because of one teacher—one teacher perceptive enough to see my gift, to know how to draw me out and give me a push—that I was finally encouraged to step outside my comfort zone and reach deeper inside myself. In the end, I kept my perfect G.P.A. and, as a bonus, my professor gladly wrote me letters of recommendation so I could transfer to another college that would allow me to split my major between photography *and* writing. And while the visual arts might have been my most natural means of expression, from that moment on, I eagerly welcomed the challenge of language and narrative—to explore my literary voice—in order to learn how to say things on paper that I wasn't able to speak.

VAYA CON DIOS
By Terri Elders

Most Golden Oldie stations don't reach further back than the early '60s, so one recent morning when Mary Ford's velvety multi-tracked voice trilled out the opening notes of *Vaya Con Dios*, I stopped sweeping the kitchen and started swaying, my broom as partner.

I had danced to this tune at a sock hop a few months into my senior year as a Manual Arts Toiler, just after my parents broke the news at Thanksgiving dinner that we were moving to Lynwood. "Our house is right across the street from Edith's," Mama said, alluding to her best friend since childhood. "And it's a five minute walk to the high school." In 1953 Los Angeles few teenagers owned cars. Moving to Lynwood, a dozen miles south, would be like moving to Mongolia.

"I'm not going to be here for the prom? Or graduation?" I dropped my fork. Mama's usually irresistible walnut stuffing held no appeal. I swabbed my napkin at the tears trickling down my cheeks.

"Lynwood High might have a prom, too," Mama said, "And quite possibly a graduation. We're not moving to another planet." I shook my head. Nothing would ever be the same. I could barely finish my pumpkin pie.

On the last Friday before Christmas vacation, I dragged through the day, from A-Period on. Not long after dawn those of us who put together the daily school newspaper, the linotype operators and page editors, gathered in the print shop for A-Period. Munching on the cafeteria's gargantuan cinnamon rolls, we pulled proofs from the trays of print, and made our last minute corrections. That year my friend Phil handled the news while I managed features.

Earlier that week the Daily had carried a paragraph Phil wrote about my transfer to Lynwood, mentioning how I'd been the B12 Class majorette, the head attorney of Girls' Court, and how I had performed in the annual assemblies of Pavlovettes, the modern dance club. He'd titled the story, "Vaya Con Dios, Terri!"

After school we crowded into the gym for the holiday hop. But on this final day at Manual, even the garlands of sparkling fairy lights failed to ignite any matching holiday twinkle in my heart. "Vaya Con Dios" had reached Number One on all the charts that month, so it was no surprise when it started up at the hop. Phil scurried across the floor. "Come on, Termite, let's shake a leg." I rose and we shuffled together in a doleful fox trot. When Mary Ford sang the line about dawn breaking through a gray tomorrow, I rested my cheek against Phil's slender shoulder and stifled a sob.

"I won't be here to help edit the Last Will and Testament for the paper," I wailed. Phil patted my back. "We'll really miss you," he said. "Vaya con dios, my darling," he sang in a teasing tone, "Vaya con dios, my love."

I started to giggle. Phil and I addressed one another by mildly insulting nicknames rather than by endearments.

"I'll miss you, too, Pencilhead," I said. "And all of my friends here, too, my darling, my love."

After the hop Phil walked me to my locker and helped me box up my belongings. "It's been great working with you these past years," he said. "You'll be amazed at what awaits you if you open your eyes and your heart."

I doubted that, but thanked him as he gave me a hug.

To my amazement, though I continued to grieve, sometimes sullenly, for the loss of my friends, Lynwood High welcomed me. When I had arrived in January 1954 my new English teacher asked if I would become copy editor for the *Accolade*, and I'd immediately agreed. I also become a feature writer for the Castle Courier, the school paper, a monthly. Manual Arts had been the only high school west of the Mississippi to publish a daily, so I was asked to speak to the beginning journalism classes about what it had been like to face constant deadlines.

In turn I eventually began to welcome life's twists, turns and transitions. My Manual Arts experience in writing against a daily deadline prepared me well for a variety of jobs that eventually took me away from Southern California and to far flung corners of the earth, even Mongolia.

In 2004 I learned that my two high schools, Manual and Lynwood, would stage their 50th reunions in Southern California on consecutive Saturdays. All those years ago I had never envisioned actually attending a 50th reunion, let alone two.

I took my *Accolade* to the Lynwood reunion. "We had such a great time getting the annual ready for the printer," one former colleague recalled. "Remember how we sat for hours on those Saturday afternoons, pouring through *Roget's Thesaurus*?"

Actually the five months had gone so fast I had almost forgotten how fun-filled the days had been. I found that being new has a special added attraction, a hint of the exotic. In suburban Lynwood I was regarded as a stranger from the strange but glamorous city of Los Angeles.

At the Manual reunion, I recognized fewer faces, and those classmates I did approach gave me blank looks. Then Phil strode into the room, looking 40 pounds heavier and 50 years grayer. I walked over to him.

"Do you remember me? Terri?"

"Of course I do, Termite," he answered. "So how did it go when you left us, whinging and whining, wailing and weeping, bawling and blubbering all the way?"

Phil had not changed. "It's been an amazing adventure these past decades," I began. "I've reinvented myself in dozens of settings, lived overseas for a decade, explored over 50 countries, and toiled all across the States."

"Was every goodbye a heartbreaker?"

"Yep," I answered truthfully. "Each and every one! But every hello was a heartwarmer."

"If you stop staring at the door that's closed, you see the one that's opened." Phil had always been wise. We chatted for an hour before saying farewell. Almost in unison we chanted, "Vaya con dios."

Back in my kitchen, Mary Ford was just finishing up. "But the memories we share are there to borrow," she harmonized with herself.

Just as there is a time to stop weeping, there is a time to stop sweeping. I two-stepped to the final echoes of the song, then brushed the kitchen crumbs into my dustbin and shoved the broom back into the closet.

NIGHT AND DAY
By Susan Mahan

My father wore pressed white shirts and bow ties.
He buffed his leather shoes to a high shine.
He was serious, thoughtful and polite,
drawing on his pipe to consider his words.
Dad wouldn't say horseshit
if he was standing in a pile of it.

My grandfather had the deepest dimples and a twinkle in his eye.
He chewed tobacco and kept a spit jar in his pocket.
Sometimes Papa Matt wore his pajamas
the whole time we were there.
Nana was always mad at him and giving him a look.
Papa Matt had a raspy Irish brogue,
and he cackled at his own stories.
His speech was peppered with occasional curses
 and words like hoodwink and malarkey.

Dad bought my sisters and me valentines every year,
signing *Love, Dad* in his meticulous left-handed cursive.
He told us stories about World War II on our daytime walks
and Aesop's fables at bedtime.
He taught me that life was tough sometimes,
but that you could get through it if you did the right thing.
My little sister said his stories were boring,
and she didn't understand
what "slow and steady wins the race" meant.

Sometimes I forgot what Dad was talking about
if he paused too long in thought,
but I had decided that my father and I were tortoises.
My sister was a hare.

Papa Matt thought it was important to pay attention
and to keep the upper hand.
His standing advice was to
answer the door with a hat and coat on.

If it was someone you liked,
you could say you had just gotten home;
if not, you could say you were on your way out.

Papa Matt taught me to be skeptical.

Dad taught me to believe.

DAD
By Paula Timpson

Dad,
first man in my life
lil' girl carried upon shoulders,
at the sea,
our favorite 'happy' place to always 'be'!
Love, so pure, is
forever
a father and daughter
as
One,
belonging
in a silly world, hearts full of fire and ideas,
hopeful ideals to create
a better world...
touching truth,
life begins
each time we
become humble and forgive,
fearless, free...
learning
how to really live
& believe !!!

PINK COCONUT SNO-BALLS
By Kellye Blankenship

He was a man of great physical strength. He was blessed with the ability to create, using the earth's surface as a canvas. He operated heavy equipment effortlessly, the dozer being his equipment of choice. The evidence of many toiling hours, fashioned his leather colored skin.

Recalling a few years back, a faint aroma of diesel and dirt enter my memories. Not necessarily a scent to be bottled for retail, but to a little girl with pigtails, not so long ago, it meant Daddy's home.

With Daddy's arrival a number of events could occur. First and foremost his lunch box would be the anticipated focal point. With any luck the summer day would be one of intense heat. Conditioning is a funny thing, but without fail, if the days were hot, daddy would usually forgo his dessert. So it didn't take me long to learn that my nightly prayers should include a heartfelt request for extreme heat.

The roar of the engine could be heard as his old diesel truck made its way up our gravel drive. Our German Shepherd, Cubby, would have the jump on me but my bare feet skimmed the gravel with little difficulty. The old metal door popped, echoing sound across the yard as he stepped out into his evening role: Daddy. I greeted him with the usual, "Let me get that for you." A gentle smile crossed his face as he handed me the small black box that had occupied my thoughts for the last hour or so. The handle was made of hard black plastic and was connected to the rounded top with metal clamps. It was usually very light in weight, so I gave him a puzzled look when I noticed its heaviness. Rubbing the top of my head, as he headed to the house, the aroma that trailed him was developing my future memories. I would only realize after many years had passed.

God had been good to me on this particular day, providing just the right amount of heat to support my anticipation with a boasting confidence. There was absolutely no way my father had eaten his dessert, and the heaviness offered additional anticipation. Though we did not share a favorite taste in desserts, I was willing to sacrifice by choking down whatever Mom had packed for him.

Big pink marshmallow balls with coconut were his favorite, they came two in a package. I'm not fond of coconut, but sometimes sacrifices have to be made.

Unbeknownst to me, my father had quickly motioned my mother to the front porch. They stood quietly observing as if Christmas morning had arrived. Sometimes words cannot be summoned to describe the profound admiration that possesses the heart of a parent. This admiration rapidly develops with no endeavor to seek an earned status from the recipient. Earned love is empty.

As I made my way across the grassy yard, I chose to sit under the large oak tree that grew very near to the chicken pen. Cubby was too hot and lazy to be interested and began sifting through a dirt pile in search of a cool place to rest. I quickly sat on my knees and placed the box flat on the grass in front of me. Before I opened the silver metal fasteners, I whispered my little daily prayer, "Please God, don't let it be those nasty pink coconut things."

As I finalized my earnest request, I opened my eyes and reached for the box. My mouth watering, I raised the lid. My eyes widened, my breath stopped and my muscles lost all function. The idea of marshmallow balls retreated as my statue demeanor bargained away my ability to react. I silently watched, while five baby skunks came to life with curiosity. Small streaks of sun peeked through the branches above, causing their soft black fur to appear wet.

With smiles as big as a parent's face can make, they slowly strolled over to ease any developed fears the new little stinkers may have allowed. My daddy had found the nest in a nearby cove where he had been clearing trees. He spared me the details of their mother but was not able to keep these little guys from touching his heart.

I proudly pointed out, I was wearing my favorite faded green shirt. The picture of three small skunks was barely visible but I still wore it as often as Mom allowed. The caption still intact, "I'm a little stinker."

So while the memory of my green shirt surfaced, he had carefully gathered my new pets, anticipating the smile they would bring. My memory bank grew. I would like to tell you I remember each of their names. I don't. But I do remember a man that worked hard, loved deeply and will never know how proud I am to be called his daughter.

My Daddy taught me many things. Most of what he taught I saw. I have seen him laugh and I have seen him cry. I watch as his eyes tell of his love while he listens to my mother. I have seen his many faces; like the one that softens with delight when his grandchildren enter the room, the one that hardens with anger when his expectations have been compromised, the one that looks intently for something to throw when frustration consumes him, the one that bows in church, showing the appropriate respect to his own father, the one that gets a glimpse of death, but turns just in time to receive the blessing of a few more days.

Many lessons learned cannot be credited to lectures of advice and knowledge. While they factor in with great value, observational lessons weigh heavily in our education.

His leather-like hands, tanned from the sun, tell a story. Palms, callused from years of determination to feed his growing family, still hold weather-beaten scars. His hair is graying now, and with each year his glasses thicken. When you visit, you may find yourself repeating an unheard statement. You see him as a man. But for a moment, let me present him as a hero, my hero.

The day will come, when the phone will ring and it won't be his voice. So I beseech you as you are blessed with one more day to pick up the phone and convey your appreciation to your hero, your teacher or to the one that influenced you by educating you with their life.

Thank you Daddy, you are my hero and I love you.

MODELING THE POSSIBLE:
AN INTERGENERATIONAL INSPIRATION
By Judy Shepps Battle

Lottie was 78 years old when she painted her first picture. Canvas, brushes, paint and smock were provided by the Jewish Home for the Aged that had been her residence for five years. The painting was a view from the beach, Coney Island in Brooklyn, and clearly communicated her awe of the mighty Atlantic Ocean.

Lottie was definitely a lifelong learner, though I doubt that she would have seen herself in this light. Like many women of her generation, she left school after eighth grade to do factory work — a job she kept until she married. She raised three children during the Great Depression and focused on feeding, clothing and educating them. All three graduated from high school.

After her husband died, she entered into an arranged marriage with a much older man — Sam — knowing her job was to care for him until his death. She did so, and a few years later voluntarily entered the Home for the Aged so as not to be a burden to her children.

It was there she discovered art and self-expression.

I suspect that Lottie was simply born at the wrong time. Latent artistic talent in a female of any age, let alone a senior citizen, was something not openly discussed and certainly not valued. Feminism was a radical idea, whispered in cultural circles that Lottie did not know existed.

Society's view of women, the aging population and the nature of learning has changed a lot since Lottie's day. While I don't know if she would have taken advantage of the many community-based classes now available in her Bensonhurst neighborhood, I like to think she would have been an avid participant.

I envision her boarding a public bus to Brooklyn Community College to take Saturday oil painting classes and eventually enrolling in one of the city colleges for a degree in the fine arts. I see her standing on the Brighton Beach boardwalk, a red beret atop her head, painting an early morning summer sunrise.

I didn't know anything about Lottie's artistic abilities until decades after her death, while clearing out my mother's apartment. Lottie was her mother — my grandmother — and the nursing home had sent the paintings after she died. The framed canvases were neatly stacked in my mother's bedroom closet, gathering dust.

Lottie was certainly no Grandma Moses. "Lots of passion but little technical ability" was the expression used by a family member to describe her work. But I have two of her paintings — the Coney Island one and a New York skyline view — next to my writing space as a reminder of my artistic legacy and my unmet responsibility to share my writings publicly.

I am walking Lottie's unfinished path today. Even though I carved out a formal career as a sociologist and psychotherapist, my passion has been writing since I was ten years of age. It is this part of my self that I have not fully honored.

As with Lottie, the society of my growing-up days did not see "writing" as a viable occupation for a woman, and I was urged to be more practical. College, graduate school, employment, and raising a family formed a seamless and breathless continuum of activity, leaving little time for reflective writing.

Still, whenever and wherever I could, I wrote. Poems, spiritual meditations, articles on learning and addictions, and even a 120-page nonfiction manuscript on teen suicide fill a four-drawer file cabinet. While a portion of this material has appeared in small literary magazines and on the Internet, much remains unpublished.

It's time that this mental roadblock, so manifest in my maternal lineage, is overcome.

There are free and low-cost classes available at the local library, senior citizens center, high school and community college. There are opportunities for me to read my poetry at open-mike sessions at local bookstores.

I can break this generational cycle of fear of owning artistic talent and passion by pursuing a Master's degree in Fine Arts at any number of excellent online, low-residency programs or by attending a variety of summer writers' conferences or applying to experience a writers retreat.

My grandmother waited until all her responsibilities were met before focusing on her inner artist. My mother, who loved words and listening to opera, never ventured down the path of artistic self-expression; her lifelong depression drained all creative energies.

The mantle of modeling creativity and loyalty to an inner muse is now on my shoulders. Hopefully, those next in line in my maternal lineage will begin the process of acting on inner loyalty, rather than on external expectations, a lot earlier than Lottie or I.

I smile at the potential snowball effect on generations yet to be born of this simple act of self-acknowledgment.

STILL AROUND
By Marsha Pearl Jamil

"How are you, Rhoda?"

"I'm still around," was always the answer in an upbeat voice filled with vitality.

One seldom had time to hear about Rhoda's problems. You were too busy answering her questions about how you were doing. She was a fantastic listener -- always asking the right questions.

If everything was going wrong in your own life, Rhoda would put the facts into perspective, and by the time you left her, you were able to see the cup half full, not half empty.

Making you feel good about yourself was Rhoda's secret recipe for friendship. When you were with her you felt clever, talented and special -- which was actually what Rhoda was - a top New York home designer who was extraordinarily bright, extraordinarily gifted, extraordinarily special.

I have terrific taste. I know this for a fact because my friend Rhoda told me so. Every time I walk into a room in my house, I feel Rhoda's presence. After nearly a quarter of a century and four additions, most of which Rhoda was involved with in one way or another, I hear her telling me how exciting this is, how perfect that is. She actually let me believe that all was a result of *my* good taste.

I don't think of Rhoda's long periods of illness. I think of her long periods of health. For despite her illnesses, she was probably one of the healthiest people I have known. I cannot remember her complaining; only stating medical fact. One was not allowed to feel sorry for Rhoda; you were too caught up in her uncanny process of celebrating life.

She is the example we use when we tell acquaintances about positive thinking, overcoming obstacles, survival not just with dignity but with élan. And yes, even miracles. It took 13 years to end a life the doctors at Sloane Kettering originally said would expire in six to eight weeks. She is a part of the best of all of us, and for me, Rhoda will always be "...still around."

HE CAME HOME
By Jan Cline

A while back, I came across a CD of photos. As I slipped the disc into my computer, I was surprised to see that they were pictures and videos my son-in-law had taken while in Iraq. I wasn't sure what I would be looking at, and was hoping I wouldn't be intruding to view them. Most of the pictures were of the countryside; a dry terrain, treeless and boring, with very little shade to offer shelter from the heat.

As I finished viewing the pictures, I thought back to all the emails we received from Jesse while he was deployed. In the beginning, the communication was meant for his family and close friends, keeping us as informed as the Army would allow. His messages were very well written, and often filled with witty stories or interesting facts about the people and culture. He withheld all the information he knew would worry his loved ones, and remained upbeat in his choice of words.

Our friends and extended family would ask about him regularly, and we would share a bit of the updates as they came. After a while, there were many requests for us to forward his emails.

It didn't take long for the word to spread, and soon Jesse's messages were linked all over the world. His writing talent and personal touch left everyone waiting with anticipation for the next email to come. We would all laugh and cry as we read. Jesse knew that people were following him and sending out prayers, but none of us really knew how many lives were touched by him. Many folks he had never met would email him with messages of encouragement and appreciation. Even now, several years later, I occasionally have someone comment on how much they enjoyed hearing from him.

As I continued to view the CD, I opened up files of videos he had taken of the area. There were several sequences of moving views out of a chopper door, where all you could hear was the loud beating of the whirling rotor blades. Then there was a guided tour of his quarters, narrated by him.

The last videos took me by surprise, and gripped my heart. They were videos of Jesse reading a story out of a children's book for his daughter, Abby. He talked to her just as if she was there, and read all her favorite stories that he read to her at home – "Good Night Moon" and "Mrs. Spider's Tea Party." My eyes filled with tears as I thought about how he must have missed his little one. This was his way of keeping her memory of him fresh, and enabled him to feel he was parenting her, even from far away. Abby loved watching the videos, and would point at the screen and say "Daddy".

For the most part he kept in close contact, but there were times when my daughter would not have any message from him for several days. He later explained that all communications were cut off when a soldier was killed, to avoid premature news leaks to the family of the deceased. After learning that, any loss of contact tested our faith, but we knew God was in control. Time seemed to drag on, but at last it was over – for our family at least. I'm so thankful that we saw a happy ending to his deployment. He made it home safely, coming home to a daughter that recognized him, and reached for him almost immediately. He came home to once again hold her in his arms, and read her all the books she loved. He came home to a family that loved him and appreciated his sacrifice. He came home to see the birth of another little girl. All those who followed him will forever cherish the emails that, for a few moments each week, took us outside of ourselves and to a land far away. His encouragement to trust God with all things spoke to all of us. His faithfulness to give glory to God for protection and grace during those difficult months left a lasting impression.

When I am tested by the trials of life I think of those long days of separation for Jesse and other men and women. Their sacrifice continues to teach us courage, and their example will stand for a new generation.

PERHAPS FORGIVENESS SUSTAINS
By Liz Rose Dolan

My god, the woman could forgive anything:
my boyfriend blotto in the lawn chair in our backyard,
his forearm gashed, his pristine Karmann Ghia totaled.
Too bad he wasn't totaled, I said
A man has to be able to take a drink, she said.
She'd tell us to respect our father after his tirade
over a missing pocket watch, *because he's your father
and you don't know everything, Miss. Your father peddled
apples during the depression.*
I arrived a decade later and she was still wetting the leaves
for his tea and peeling the spuds for his supper.
She even forgave God for taking four children:
each night on her callused knees, her crystal rosaries
shackling her hands folded on the chenille spread.
Above her bowed head,
Magdalene Touching the Foot of the Cross.
Perhaps forgiveness sustains.
At ninety-six, still sharp, after relishing a chicken salad sandwich,
Mother died,
her heart still as big as a blue whale's.

HONING THE HULA
By Meredith Escudier

Hula dancing was not part of the fourth grade curriculum at my elementary school in California. In those days, the early fifties, Hawaii had not even gained official statehood yet. It seemed as remote as Fiji to me, as entrancing as a foreign tongue, as faraway as the glossy photographs from the *National Geographic*. Nevertheless, my heart would embrace all things Hawaiian that year, as I was graced by what seemed like Honolulu's loveliest ambassador: My teacher, Miss Ho.

Young, attractive and Chinese-Hawaiian, Miss Ho migrated into my existence like an exotic tropical bird, one that I might possibly emulate, I thought, no matter how far-fetched that achievement would be for a Caucasian nine-year-old wearing sensible, white Oxfords on her growing feet. But alert to her every move, I kept careful watch of her conversational tics, her sense of humor and her fashion choices (white drip-dry blouse, belted skirt), hoping against hope to soak up some lesson on how to be a person...ideally a person quite like her.

She was new to our school and swelled the ranks of an already fully feminine teaching staff. The only grown-up male presence was our principal, whom we glimpsed during his occasional appearances on the playground. Girls flocked around him, recklessly abandoning a game of four-square or a tight tetherball match only to flutter about in misguided affection and Pope-like reverence. But I refrained from such overstatement, sensing no need to honor him. I had my teacher to venerate instead...and the hula as yet to master. Miss Ho had promised to teach us the elusive dance and by April, we knew the end-of-year program was drawing near.

Oh, my yellow ginger lei sang a soulful Hawaiian tenor to the strains of the ukulele. Left-together-left, I repeated under my breath... *reveals its scent through the day...* the recorded voice sang on, unperturbed by the girls in our class standing in parallel rows behind Miss Ho's petite silhouette. Valiant in our attempts to imitate the sequence of her footwork, we added airy hand and arm motions. Waving repeatedly in rhythmic motion, we set about to tackle that most challenging of tasks for our androgynous bodies, the swaying of our so-called hips. When Miss Ho slipped off her mid-heeled leather pumps in her need to get it right, her stocking feet said it all. The key to the hipwork was in the footwork. Eureka! Freed at last from these Oxfords, I would stretch out my toes, play with my freshly liberated arches and place the weight of my undulating body on the balls of my feet where it belonged. My grass skirt would sway languorously in the breeze, a tropical sunset appearing as backdrop. *My heart is yearning for you.* With time and practice, I reasoned, my emancipated limbs and curling toes would be able to scale, say, a coconut tree, something really useful for any fourth-grader. The image of my sprightly skills came as a pleasing one as did the prospect of the many leis we would be making for the performance. Ginger blossoms being in short supply, tissue paper would have to do, laboriously fashioned into peach-colored flowers. Good enough.

Miss Ho's class of 28 pupils included 13 boys. Hula would not be their thing, they were relieved to know, but native Hawaiian dance was rich in masculine narrative as well, she told them, and throwing caution to the winds, she provided each boy with two-colored percussion sticks. Despite the clear and constant risk of their riotously clobbering each other over the head at any moment, she taught them a Stick Dance. They absorbed it all: the steps, the beat, the leaps and the whoops, rehearsing breathlessly in their plaid shirts and turned-up denim jeans while scuffing up the floor in their Buster Brown shoes.

It took a large stretch of the imagination to see us as emissaries of native Hawaiian culture, but hours of concentration and unmitigated desire had somehow transformed us into Miss Ho's freckled and funny-faced Ballet Folklorico. On the day of the performance, the girls swayed their hips in studious concentration, wearing whatever colorful skirt could possibly lend itself to a luau-type event, and the boys jumped around wildly, their flailing arms chopping the air in chaotic clicking stick rhythm on an unrelenting background of chanted staccato Hawaiian syllables. The audience of parents, grateful for the absence of major mishaps, applauded thunderously, animated by the enthusiasm genetically programmed into proud parents. Magic. Miss Ho's fourth graders were all slightly Hawaiian that day as all those present, pupils and parents alike, became accomplices in the tacit decision to dismiss the glaring evidence to the contrary, offered up in brazen abandon.

Looking back, I'm sure Miss Ho must have also taught us fractions that year. There were undoubtedly units on science and social studies. Chapters were read. Comprehension questions got done. I may have been a finalist in a Spelling Bee or two.

But Miss Ho's enduring legacy for me would lie elsewhere, in the artistry of transmitting a bit of culture completely outside of the curriculum's requirements for minimum achievement. I learned that the world was large, replete with riches, possibly exotic and most certainly beckoning. *My heart is yearning for you....*

DUTY
By Skip Hughes

"I did my duty," the old man said,
"But I always loved, purely loved to fly,
And there never was anywhere flying like that,
Shot from a gun off a carrier deck.

"Strapped in tight on the catapult,
Helmet and head squeezed back to the pad,
Engine screaming, watch for the signal,
One long WHAM! And I'd be flying.

"Now's the busy time. Clean up the airplane:
Rack the landing gear out of the slipstream,
Notch up the flaps as she gains her speed,
And feel the wheels thump into their wells.

"Then skim low and fast above the water.
Pull straight up in a vertical climb,
Light off the burner, and scram for the sky
Like a homesick angel. That, is flying.

"Our missions were short, an hour at most.
Every launch, I would have this awful thought.
'What if I don't come back today?
What's Janie to do? How about the kids?'

"Then, 'Oh well. I get to fly today,
And there's duty, there's duty to be done.'
So I flew and I fought, and I kept coming back.
With Jake on my wing, we looked out for each other.

"I remember that day. I remember it well,
Still over the target, but ordnance expended
And turning away to head for home,
When I heard it and felt it, and I knew I was hit.

"Jake pulled in tight, and I heard him say,
'Climb while you can and head for the coast.
Over open water, your pick-up will be
So quick you almost won't get wet.'

"I did what I could, but she wouldn't respond.
'Keep flying, old girl. Get me feet-wet at least.'
'No good,' I radioed to Jake,
'Stay with me, Buddy. I've got to punch out.'

"That ejection sequence is one hell of a ride.
The straps grabbed on tight like a big jungle snake.
The canopy blew loose, and then came the kick
When the seat blasted me slap out of the airplane.

"That seat popped my chute when it pushed me away.
I was high enough to see the water,
But too low to get there by parachute.
So I hung in the sky and got shot at there.

"I knew my pick-up was on its way.
There'd be fighters orbiting overhead,
As the helos hovered to pluck me out,
And maybe, maybe they'd be quick enough.

"I must have landed in a banana plantation.
That part of the story is good for a laugh,
But I broke a leg and arm when I hit.
They had me so fast, there would be no rescue."

He doesn't discuss what happened then,
Or the seven years he was prisoner of war.
Seven years ripped harshly out of his life,
And his family's life too, just gone forever.

He was debriefed of course, so the Navy knows,
And we know enough about the brutality.
His rehab was hard, and he took some time
To become a husband and father again.

He skippered a carrier, got promoted Admiral,
Still flew when he could, even after he retired.
He was always a source of inspiration
To his family, to the sailors he commanded.

I have never met a more civilized person,
Honest, genuine, thoughtful, and kind.
He had taken the measure of human suffering,
And nothing could bother him after that.

He did his duty, and that was plenty.
He said, "A man needs to do what he can,
Perhaps to make his world a better place,
But try, try hard not to make it worse."

OY, THE RUST IN THE GOLDEN YEARS
By Constance Gilbert, RNC-retired

Our lives are filled with people, who cross our path and affect our lives in small yet sometimes, lasting ways. "Grandma" was one of my path-crossers.

An 80-plus, Dutch woman phoned one afternoon saying, "It's time. I'm moving there tomorrow." I was speechless for a moment. You just don't call up and request a bed with a window facing the front, as if making hotel reservations. In a gentle way, I tried to explain the procedures for admission, including the fact that SummerHouse Care Center* had few openings and a bed by the window was rarely available for new residents. The woman firmly, but sweetly told me to take care of it; she'd see me in the morning.

This Dutch lady had no family. She had sold her home a few years before, and moved into the apartments near the care center in preparation for the day when she could no longer manage on her own. Thus, "I'll be there in the morning. And, oh... just call me 'Grandma'."

At mid-morning, "Grandma" arrived. She knew exactly what she was doing. And she was not the confused woman I envisioned. Actually, she was woman of great faith and even greater tenacity. "A bed would be ready, when the Good Lord was ready for me to move," she declared. End of discussion.

Within a few hours, SummerHouse became Grandma's new mission. At first, we didn't realize that she'd adopted each of us as her family—her children. Her pleasant Dutch accent; sparkling eyes that missed nothing; crown of pure white hair; and subtle sense of humor charmed everyone she met. Her body was wearing out, but not her spirit.

No day was wasted. As active as her body allowed, Grandma joined into the life of SummerHouse with a happiness and energy that was contagious. It wasn't long before she knew the staff and all the patients, along with their families and friends— people needing encouragement, advice or even a reprimand. They were drawn to her enchanting, affectionate demeanor.

Old-fashioned, and proud of it, Grandma counseled many declaring marriage as sacred—living together was not a true commitment. Divorce was a cop-out. "Takes hard work to be happily married," she'd say. Letting a man abuse you was not to be tolerated;

and parenting didn't include bar hopping. Furthermore, we must live each day, as if it was our last.

It always tickled me when the staff complained to Grandma about too much work. Firmly, she described working in a factory when she was barely four years old: "I stood on a stool for eight hours a day on an assembly line with my Mama. Now *that* was hard work."

She was aglow with love and understanding, even when expressing her disapproval. More than anything, everyone wanted to please Grandma. Just being with her, we tried to absorb her very essence and yearned for her peacefulness.

Stop by and you'd find her arthritic fingers busy with a ball of white thread and a crochet hook making crosses, or holding someone's hand. She traveled from room to room, via wheelchair, sharing her quick wit and her joy for life. When there was a need, she'd have an aide escort her to a hurting visitor or a dying patient; or she would summon a staff member to drop by "for a chat." Even when she became bed-bound, she continued to crochet white crosses to give away, and draw people to her.

Her well worn Bible was always close at hand; but she never preached, rarely quoted Scripture and no one ever *saw* her praying. Yet, all knew each stitch was a prayer for the person the cross would be given to. Her every breath was a prayer and her life said more than words ever could.

One afternoon, Grandma's ball of thread unraveled as it crossed the hall right in front of me. Retrieving it, I began rolling the thread around the vagrant ball. I continued to concentrate on a solution to my latest dilemma.

"Must be difficult to crochet when you lose your thread," I said entering her room.

Grandma smiled. Then she paused between stitches . . . "It wasn't lost. I sent it out to get you." Aha, it was my turn. Actually, she was concerned about one of my nursing assistants. I left 20 minutes later knowing why I loved my job. Also, a solution for my problem came to mind as I exited her room. Coincidence? I don't think so.

Months later: "Grandma wants you." As I entered her room, her eyes still held a sparkle as her fingers drew the crochet hook in and out. "Pass me the scissors," was all she said. Knowing I was summoned for a reason, I watched and waited. She'd tell me in her time and in her own way. She snipped the thread. Then placing the eight inch, white cross near her heart, she slowly smoothed it out. "I saved the last one for you," she said softly.

"Your work's completed?" We both knew it wasn't really a question, but she nodded. I held the cross, missing her already, and I, too, nodded. No other words were needed. Just like the day she first phoned, she knew when it was time to move on.

The balls of thread and crochet hooks were put away. She had finished so much more than the crosses. Quietly, during her remaining days and hours, all of the staff visited her. Some stopped in for a last word of advice. All, to say good-bye and thank you.

"Be good and be about His business," she whispered to each one.

At about the same time in the morning, as the day she arrived, she left us. I think I heard the swoosh of angel wings and wondered who was giving the directions. I wept, but also felt the joy of being a part of her life. It was an honor and a privilege to call her "My Grandma."

The ripple-effect of this Dutch woman cannot be measured. Our staff and residents alone numbered nearly 150 each day. She touched thousands of hearts and souls in the brief time I knew her. She's proof that our life does not depend on where we are, how old or young we are, the right timing, who crosses our path, or how we feel. With a servant's heart, Grandma was true to her faith—in people and in God. For to Grandma, each day was a gift to be shared.

Now, I have rust in my golden years, but she prepared me for it. Her precious "last cross" is my daily reminder to grasp every opportunity each day brings.

Oh, that my legacy may be like the Dutch lady who once said, "I'll be there in the morning. And just call me Grandma."

A PASSIONATE TEACHER
By Barbara Mayer

A born teacher, my friend Monica motivates, inspires and makes learning fun. When other teachers have given up on a student, she finds the key to help each one succeed. Whether they are discipline problems, slow learners, or behind in their skills, she helps them feel good about themselves and overcome the obstacles to their learning.

Monica teaches communication arts to fifth and sixth graders at a large Midwestern school. She also tutors children after school and sometimes at her home on weekends. "I worry about children who are behind in their skills," she said. "It is easier to correct a deficiency in grade school and give them a solid foundation for learning in their high school years. Besides, the earlier one can remediate, the less of a burden for society."

Using simple number games, she can teach math at any level. The word failure is not in her vocabulary. She believes every child can learn – a teacher just has to find what motivates each one.

"Some children are more visual learners, some are more auditory," she explains. "I just use as many of the senses and hands-on activities as I can to teach abstract concepts."

Monica loves children and they know it immediately. She praises them for each success they experience and makes them eager to learn more. She truly believes that "nothing succeeds like success."

Jacob is one example. He had fallen behind in his math and couldn't seem to catch up. His parents asked Monica to tutor him. When he came for his first session, his head was down and shoulders slumped. He didn't like having to be tutored and he felt like he was beyond help. After several months, he was coming in with smiles and a bounce in his step. The difference? Monica instilled confidence and believed in him. He was learning how to multiply and divide whole numbers and fractions. He found out it was fun and he began to look forward to his tutoring sessions.

"I wish you could be my teacher forever," he tells her.

"Oh, pretty soon you won't need me anymore," she says with a grin. "You're getting smarter than I am."

Kyle is another example. He had been out of school for awhile because his parents had divorced and he had been shipped to his grandparents. He was several grade levels behind in reading and math.

He was a discipline problem and his teacher yelled at him. Monica took him under her wing and he began to blossom. After a year of extra help he was outshining the other students.

He recently called Monica to tell her his news, his voice bursting with excitement. "I was the only one in my class who got a 100 on my history test," he said.

"I'm not surprised, Kyle, I'm very proud of you," she said.

Recently a fifth grader came to Monica in tears because she didn't know her multiplication tables. "Give me 15 minutes after school for three weeks and she'll know them," Monica told her mother. At the end of three weeks she took the happy student to the Dairy Queen to celebrate her success.

Monica puts all the times tables on a chart and as a student learn them, the student crosses them off with a colored pen. She also gives timed tests to let them see their progress. To teach percentages, Monica takes children to the store to look for sales. When something is marked 15% or 25% off, she makes them figure out how much it will cost. She also takes them to the bank to get money and then to the grocery store to buy something and calculate the sales tax. "I have them compare how much candy they can get for $5 and how much fruit for the same price and which is better for you," she explains. "I don't reward them with candy; instead I give them praise and let them write their own A on their papers."

To teach area, she has them measure their bedrooms and estimate how much paint to buy for the walls and how much carpeting they would need for the floor. To teach measurements, she uses milk cartons to show pints and sticks of oleo to show tablespoons as they bake brownies.

"I try to help them see how important math is in their everyday lives," Monica said.

Monica is now in her 60s but her energy and enthusiasm have not diminished. She is always on the alert for teaching materials and uses much of her own money to buy what she thinks will help children learn. But most of her tools come from newspapers, libraries, and household items. Her best reward is to see new concepts click in the student's mind that shows he or she "got it."

"Children are our greatest resource and it is our privilege to insure they achieve," she said. "We cannot afford to let them fail. They are our future and the world needs bright, intelligent and creative leaders."

Monica attributes her love of teaching to the Benedictine Sisters who taught her in grade school, high school and college. "They were great teachers and I owe my education and passion for learning to them, as well as my family," she says.

Although she has never had children of her own, this teacher cares about her students as if they were her own. She loves to watch them change and grow. Parents are always grateful and amazed at what she is able to accomplish with their children.

I have learned so much from watching Monica work with children. Her creativity and genuine concern for each child have made me a more empathetic teacher.

TRIVIAL PURSUITS
"Men consider what women do as trivial" - Lucille Clifton
By Ben Humphrey

Advanced degrees, post graduate training,
she had these but I never heard Mom
lament her choice of motherhood to me.

She sat knitting by the piano as
I ran scales, worked the chords,
hammered away at Mozart.

Third grade teacher said: "He can't
read. We'll have to hold him
back." Mom replied: "Retest him in the fall."
She whisked me home to work

on phonics. Each day she patiently laid the cards
before me. "Ould" words: could, should, would.
All the "ing" words: ring, thing, sing. Daunting

for a dyslexic boy. Decades later
a Professor at the podium, I knew
my mom, the architect, had laid the foundation
for me: academia, productivity, music.

OBEDIENCE AND WILLINGNESS
By Naty Matos

I have had several people who have inspired me throughout my life, but I have to say that one that has made a recent and great impact is my good friend Carrie.

Carrie is a very talented woman, more than she may realize at times. She's very loving, charismatic and funny. We met through a common friend who thought that we would have compatible personalities and exchanged our phone numbers. That same week I went to lunch with her; nothing was ever the same.

From that first lunch, I knew there was something different about her. She was easy to talk to and very funny. Carrie came into my life at one of my lowest points. God placed her there in the nick of time as he always does. I honestly don't know why, but I was comfortable enough on that first meeting to tell her the circumstances that I was enduring at that time. She just smiled at me and reassured me that everything was going to be alright. She had been through some of the same struggles I was encountering and understood where I was coming from. From that day, she promised to be there for me.

In the course of my life I've had a lot of people promise me things, but most ended up with empty promises. The reality was that I didn't expect anything different from this stranger who was promising support when she barely knew me. Was I in for a real surprise?

A few days after that meeting, several things transpired. I was enduring one of the scariest nights of my life and I didn't know where to turn. I was unable to call anyone because my safety could have been compromised, so I decided to send Carrie a text message letting her know what was going on. I wanted her to respond, but I didn't expect it. After all it was two in the morning and she barely knew me. She later told me that God had woken her up because she heard her phone ring, like a phone call had come through instead of a text message. She immediately called me. Hearing her voice on the phone was very comforting, it gave me the sense that I was not alone. She guided me through the process of getting things to a stable place.

After those events, Carrie has continued her friendship with me. She has continued to be my support and inspiration. She has taken the time to learn who I am and guide me on the right path to recovery. She is teaching me how to set up healthy boundaries and enforce them. The difference between what is my responsibility and what is someone else's accountability. She's also shown me how to see myself through God's eyes instead of mine. One of the biggest lessons that I learned from her is that taking care of me is not a selfish act, but something that God wants me to do. She's truly an inspiration, as a woman and as a friend.

God has taken the opportunity of utilizing some of my experiences and has placed others in my life in need of help or at least a listening ear. Carrie taught me through her example that by being obedient in the service to those people who God has assigned to you; you are doing God's work and you are blessed in the midst of it. She has shown me that the greatest reward in fellowship is support.

Even without a word or a gesture Carrie keeps teaching me things. I have been watching her make amazing progress in her own life; she has inspired me into realizing that God can do extraordinary things when we submit to his will. She's a loving wife and mother. She has lost over 90 pounds in less than a year. She has been nicotine free for over nine months. She leads a recovery group for women with all sorts of addictions through Celebrate Recovery and sponsors about four women on their road to recovery. She is a true inspiration.

I'm far from recovered from my recent events, but God has already entrusted me with some people around me with hurts very similar to mine and I've been able to bring a ray of light to their darkest times. I have been able to offer the support that was and still is being offered to me. I have been able to see how God never wastes a hurt or pain, and not only makes us better, but teaches us how to show others the road home. I have learned to see myself through God's eyes and I'm working on waiting on his timelines. Carrie showed me the blueprint of how to do that for others, by doing it for me.

BEFORE SHE SAID GOODBYE
By Jessica Katsonga Phiri

After my parents divorced, we moved a lot. It didn't matter which parent I lived with, we moved a lot. By the time I met Mrs. Twait, I had been to eight different schools and had moved 13 times. I managed to stay on the honor roll most of the time. Mrs. Twait was a speech teacher and I happened to love speech class. I didn't care that most of the students at that school hated me with a venom I had never seen before.

The year before, I was greeted every morning by the word "Faggot" scribbled on my locker. In determinant pride, I'd walk to the office and insist that it be cleaned off before I'd go to class. I looked different than them, which was apparently a crime. It was a small town school in the middle of cornfields, saddled on a cemetery.

I had come from a bigger school with a more diverse culture. A short hair cut on a girl didn't make her gay or anything else. In fact, I had a lot of friends at my old school. I missed it there. Even the teachers at this school disliked me. One made comments about my clothes. Another harassed me every single day. He didn't like my thoughts on war and made sure that I knew it. At one point he started charging me money for leaving my computer disk in the computer when the bully behind me kept shutting off my computer throughout class and I'd give up.

Mrs. Twait was different. She'd talk to me about the future and her big green-blue eyes would smile at me over her freckled cheeks. She was young and the place hadn't killed her yet. Once, she showed me her doll. Inside one of her drawers, she reached in and plucked out a "Darnit" doll. It had a little poem on it about getting mad and smacking the doll on the desk and saying "Darnit, darnit, darnit!" We took turns using it a couple times.

Ten years later, I was a single mother with a 2-year-old little girl. I lived only blocks away from that horrible school. I missed Mrs. Twait and decided to steel my insides and go for a visit. I put the little lady in a stroller and walked in the autumn sun. She greeted me with surprise and joy. While we talked a shy young lady, came up and half-whispered to Mrs. Twait a thank you for giving her a bag of clothes. She hadn't changed at all.

It turns out Mrs. Twait, Bonnie to me, had beat cancer six times already. Her hair was a short fuzz but her smile cut through the pain. She asked about my family, each sibling, by name and I filled her in on the updates. When she asked if I'd gone to college, I looked at the floor.

"I want to, but I don't know what to go for," I admitted.

She didn't miss a beat. "Go for anything. Just go. You're too smart not to. Don't cheat yourself." She was both serious and heartfelt and I knew she was right. I had to go.

After the visit, I enrolled in college. It wasn't easy at all. I had a 2-year-old, a job and lots and lots of car problems, but I determined in my heart that I would finish. Halfway through, I got a call. Mrs. Twait had passed away. I was devastated. Only in her forties, she died without having children of her own; a dream stolen from her by cancer.

I went to my desk, a small white computer desk, I'd found on the curb and brought home after starting school. I wrote her a poem. I'd give it to her. The viewing was horrible. Students of all ages lined the hallways all the way out the door. The line to see her trailed out of the room. I tearfully greeted people I hadn't seen in years. Mrs. Twait had touched so many people, it was clear.

When I approached the casket, I held my poem tight. I leaned over to tell her "Thank you." I wanted to thank her for loving me when no one else did. I wanted to thank her for believing in me. To my surprise, a little drawer was pulled out over her hands and it was filled with other notes. *Such a short life and yet so much to take with her.*

It took me six years to earn a Bachelor's degree. I plan on returning to school to earn a teaching certificate so that I can teach English. I stop to wonder what my life would be like without Bonnie. I met my husband while doing a homework assignment. I now have a second child and a life that is overflowing with love and the satisfaction of accomplishment. God uses people and I hope and pray that God will use me in the same way he used Mrs. Twait. She was a light in the dark places for so many.

COLLEGE DAYS
By Dale S. Johnson

I dropped my daughter Khristyn off to attend college at Tuskegee University in Tuskegee, Alabama today and started on my long drive back home to Woodbury, Minnesota, just outside of St. Paul. I am so very proud of her. My little girl is getting set for her very first day of college and all that brings with it. She is a very special young lady for so many reasons, least of which is beginning what is really her "second" first day of college. Her first, first day of college actually occurred in June 2008. That college experience was cut short in August of that year by an illness that caused her to spend four months in the hospital, including two weeks in ICU, undergo five brain operations, two other surgeries, and more than seven months of rehabilitation.

In May 2008, at the age of 17, Khris graduated high school in Lithonia, Georgia and in June 2008 had begun classes at Kentucky State University (KSU) in Frankfort, Kentucky. When I had asked her why she chose KSU, she said that not only did it offer degrees in her chosen professions of psychology and journalism, but also the school was almost the exact distance between me in Chicago and her mother in Atlanta. In late July 2008 while walking to class one morning she noticed a stiffness in her right leg that was making it difficult for her to walk. By August her walking had become so restricted that she was not able to participate in a number of activities on campus. Her mother and I converged on Frankfort and took her to physicians, had x-rays done on her leg and even had a brain scan with no diagnosis determined. Khristyn finished the semester and on her return to the Atlanta area met with a neurologist who determined that she had a condition called Chiari Malformation.

Chiari malformations (CMs) are structural defects in the cerebellum, the part of the brain that controls balance. It can cause a range of symptoms including dizziness, muscle weakness, numbness, vision problems, headache, and problems with balance and coordination. Khris had Type II of this condition, which includes a form of spina bifida, a condition where the spinal canal and backbone do not close before birth and causes the spinal cord to protrude through an opening in the back. This can cause partial or complete paralysis below the spinal opening.

On September 21, 2008 Khris had what would be the first of six skull, spinal and brain operations over the next four months. She spent Thanksgiving, her birthday and Christmas of 2008 in the hospital. She was discharged shortly after Christmas. Through all those events part of her spirit stayed on her plan of returning to school. During her hospitalization she continuously texted and spoke to the friends she had made at KSU, but had decided that when she returned to school it would be a college closer to her home in Atlanta – yet, not too close. By the time she was discharged in December 2008 not only had she narrowed her choices down to Albany State, North Carolina A&T, and Tuskegee but had also applied for scholarships and financial aid packages.

Khris has always counted her family as her number two blessing behind her love of God. Her mother and I adopted Khris when she was 12 weeks old; and from that moment she entered our lives, we gave her to God and she has accepted him in return. She has also been blessed to have family and friends who had attended college. Listening to their stories and experiences she decided early on that she wanted to live and be a part of the college experience, to make her own memories of a college life.

In January 2009 Khris began her regimen of rehabilitation treatments which basically entailed teaching the right side of her body how to function again. I kid her that she went into the hospital as a right-handed person and came out a lefty as she has even taught herself how to write using her left hand. Khris walks better but she still utilizes her walker or her cane to move from class to class, and she will need a scooter to get from her dorm to buildings where her classes will be held. She has a brace on her leg that causes her discomfort if she walks too long; but she laughs and smiles with the ease of a child on her first day of school. I can see the look in her eyes wishing that she could move around with the grace of the other students on campus, but. I also catch the determination in her spirit as she perseveres through her current condition. I know that there will be times when she is alone in her dorm room that she will allow herself to embrace the pity that others oftentimes too easily cast in her direction, but she always finds her way out of those moments.

So as I head north already, scheduling my next trip south, tears fill my eyes and prayers enter my heart for my daughter and for all our family and friends who have supported her. I also bring with me an absence of concern for all those little daily irritants that clog my day. Words like "can't" and "impossible" suddenly have far less meaning then they used to have with me. I now have a new appreciation for what is truly important in my days. The one thing all real heroes have in common is that they never ask to be heroes. To my hero Khristyn, know that you are truly a gift of God to all that enter your spirit. Go Tigers!!

SURVIVAL
By Robert D. Fertig

In 1934 a family doctor, responding to a frightened mother's telephone call, came quickly to her house to check on a little boy who had fainted in the bathroom. In those days doctors made house calls. After examining the boy, the physician quickly went to the telephone to call for an ambulance and to advise the hospital of the need for immediate surgery. Then he told the little boy's mother that her son had a ruptured appendix and that surgery had to be performed immediately.

When the boy and his Mother arrived at the hospital, all was prepared. In the elevator leading up to the operating room, the little boy was asked his name, address, and names of his parents, information the hospital had to have before the emergency surgery could be performed. As soon as the incision was made by the surgeon, it was discovered that there was peritonitis in the stomach and throughout the entire gastro-intestinal system. This was before the advent of sulfa drugs and because of that, the potential for survival was close to zero. The little boy was about to learn his first lesson in survival.

After the operation and release from intensive care, the boy's first conscious thoughts were more of thirst than hunger. He kept hoping that soon they will allow him to have something to eat, or better still, have something to drink. Complaining or whining was absolutely forbidden at home. His only relief was having his lips caressed with a wet cotton swab. The nurses kept promising that he would soon have some water. He waited. "Hang on," he kept telling himself, "Do not give up. You survived the surgery. You will survive the thirst." He refused to cry. After about ten days without any food or liquids, he was given a little water to quench his overwhelming thirst. Then, at last, food! He was promised a meal which turned out to be a single leaf of iceberg lettuce. Today, raw vegetables would be frowned upon for a first meal as they are not that easily digested, but putting that aside, that single leaf of lettuce was his very first food in approximately two weeks tasting better than a double chocolate ice cream sundae.

For the better part of one year, life for the little boy consisted of his lying in bed with many tubes attached to his body, whose purpose was to drain the killing peritonitis from his system. When he was strong enough to sit up, it was decided that he could continue with school, even though his classroom was a hospital ward. Fortunately he was blessed with a teacher who came to the hospital once a week for personal hands-on instruction, testing and support. God bless teachers who have that kind of a total commitment to their students, especially that one. The little boy was determined to keep up with class work. Each day he labored with geography, history, mathematics and English. On the afternoon his teacher came, they reviewed what he had learned and what was to be learned during the following week. With the hands-on, two-hour weekly sessions with his teacher, he managed to keep up with his lessons.

Because he had been bed-ridden for almost one year, he was not aware that he had to learn to walk all over again. "Today we are going to begin to learn how to walk," a nurse said to him one day. "I don't need any lessons. Of course I can walk," responded the frightfully thin, little boy. In his manly attempt to prove it, the boy slipped over the side of the bed, put his feet on the floor, and instantly collapsed. After all of the months in bed, his weakened legs had a long way to go before they were strong enough to hold up his slight weight. By now, even with his few years of life, the little boy had learned his first lesson in never yielding to adversity. Determined not to give in, he gritted his teeth and willed himself to walk. With the nurse's help he managed two or three steps, on that first day. From then on, each day, with the help of a nurse, he stumbled a few more steps. Every day he walked just a bit further, until he was strong enough to walk on his own. Soon he could walk to the bathroom all by himself. What a relief that was. No more bed pans! Soon he was able to walk at least two times a day and learned that walking was the key to building strength and eventual release from the hospital.

This first lesson in survival was one he would use time and time again in the years to come. Never giving up, no matter what the odds were against survival. No crying. Never, not once did he cry. His objective was as pure as his innocence. Survival. Never, never, never give up! In those years there were few known survivors of that kind of peritonitis and therefore odds that he had faced were astronomical. Determination and the will never to yield, no matter what the circumstances, were the lessons now chiseled into the bedrock of that little boy.

Finally strong enough to leave the hospital and go home, he refused to be wheeled to the hospital entrance. Too proud to do otherwise, he walked out of the hospital under his own power.

His persistence and positive attitude had paid off. He had kept up with his school work while in the hospital and the recovery period at home. After an absence of one full year, he returned to school where the major highlight was being promoted, along with his fellow classmates, to the next grade. He had accomplished his required schoolwork through the encouragement of a dedicated teacher and survived by his own determination never to yield to adversity, no matter how threatening. His experiences had created in him a positive attitude towards life and the will to overcome - anything.

    That little boy was me.

MARTIN LUTHER KING JR
By Justin Blackburn

He was only a human like me or you
only he drew his breath from the spirit well of truth
and everywhere he went his breath blew the wind

He dreamed the same dream as me or you
only he knew if his dream was going to come true
he was going to have to do something about it

Yes he had people trying to rip apart the seams of his dream
but he knew love and had the belief
that one day all mankind will be free
and that was all Martin's eyes could see

He grew wings in the face of slaughter
he brought love to his enemy's daughter
he was soft while they searched him with fire
while his church burned he sang in the choir

He was only a human like you or me
only he knew equality and truth to be more important than anything
and he gave his life to that fact

When I think about him today
I feel his irresistible love and grace
I know there is nothing that can take him away from truth's place

MY OWN RACE
By Rebekah Crain

While stretching for another cross country race my teammates and I were scoping out our opponents. "I hope she doesn't beat me," my teammate Katie said wrinkling her nose at one girl.

"I'll never beat her," I said eyeing another who was built like an elite marathoner.

Coach walked by our circle and stepped inside. He reminded us this was an easy course, "But that doesn't mean you can relax out there; this is still a race, so run the way you know how." So far that season we were undefeated in our league.

"After you're done remember to stretch and do your sets of push-ups and sit-ups as usual." I thought he was finished and turned to my friend to comment, but he started again. "When you're running, don't pick out people to beat. You don't know anything about those other racers, if they're having a good day and are on top of their game or not. You know how well you can run, so you're racing against the clock. Don't worry about the people around you." He paused for emphasis and then walked away.

Katie shrugged, "I still hope she doesn't beat me."

"Don't worry about it," I said. I thought about the girl who looked like a runner. I wondered how fast she was. I glanced at the other team and wondered what they were thinking as they checked us out; who were they afraid of losing to and who did they assume they could never beat? I reached down for my toes, maybe it didn't matter, I knew how fast I was, no matter what anyone else out there did I just had to try for my personal best that day and then the next. I may not win, but hopefully, I would always improve.

I don't remember how the race went that day, or how I finished in the plethora of races I ran after that. I do know Coach's speech gave sense of focus to my running that carried me out of high school and beyond college. Incidentally I did win a few races when I was in my early twenties. I loved those moments, not because of the medals, but because each win was a new personal record. I loved getting faster and then pushing for a new goal. Even when I was in the lead I still heard Coach's voice reminding me, "Don't look behind you; check your watch." And yet there was a weight in that speech that went beyond the track and into life.

My first year of marriage was rough, after about six months sparks flew like firecrackers. My husband and I could barely find peace. He got frustrated at the situation and said, "No other couples have this many problems so soon. It isn't normal to live like this."

I told him, "How do you know that? I'm sure if anyone is having these problems they're not bragging about them." But then I said," Why are you worried about them anyway? This is us, our marriage. We can't compare ourselves to anyone, but us."

He had no response and that didn't solve the problem, but we're still married and working on staying that way. I have also been accused of being lenient in the way I raise my daughter and I respond, "Just because I don't do things the way your mother or even my mother did them, doesn't mean I'm doing it wrong. It's just different." I know that's Coach's influence.

Because I can block people out doesn't mean I'm not competitive; I'm as competitive as the next person, if not a little bit more, but I know where I've been and where I'm going. I haven't traveled anyone else's path and nobody else has traveled mine. I have no reason to pick people to watch or beat. We all have our own journeys, maybe we'll inspire each other, but we have to know when we're running a good race by our own standards, not by those of the person beside us.

THE HAT
By Elynne Chaplik-Aleskow

It started as a typical first class session of the new semester at Wright College in Chicago. Twenty-five faces were staring at me with the fear of college students who would prefer to be anywhere in the world other than a communication class. As I looked back at them with all the empathy I could express, I asked that everyone wearing hats please remove them. They looked at me with that confusion of a generation unfamiliar with such etiquette.

The hats were removed except for one young man's. When I asked him directly, he answered "No." I was shocked but did not show it. Not ten minutes into the session and in front of new students whom I was meeting for the first time, I was being challenged. How I handled this moment could determine semester survival. My semester survival.

The students were intently watching me and waiting. It was my move. I decided not to deal publicly with this challenge to my authority so I asked to see the young man after class. His name was Mark and he looked like the most unlikely of all the students to express insubordination. He was slight in build, clean cut with a pleasant face. He was not someone who stood out among the others. Yet he had said "no" to a directive from his new professor in front of new classmates on the first day of the new semester. There would be no choice. I had to convince him to do what the others were asked. He would have to back down.

After class, alone in my classroom, Mark and I faced one another. His eyes focused toward the floor. He would not look at me as I spoke. His hat, the symbol of his defiance, still sat securely on his head.

"Mark," I said softly, "you must follow the rules of this class. Removing your hat demonstrates respect. Is there a reason you feel you must wear your hat? I am willing to listen."

Mark lifted his eyes and looked into mine. "No," he answered. His look was empty. His tone was flat.

"Then you must remove it," I answered in my most professorial voice. He did as I asked.

At that moment I recognized my challenge with this young man. He complied in removing his hat but I had not reached him. I had forced him but I had not persuaded him.

Slowly throughout the semester, I felt a bond growing between Mark and me. Sometimes he would even smile at my jokes and ask thoughtful questions in class. When I saw him in the hall, he would tip his hat. I would not let him see me smile at that obvious gesture.

The final week of the semester Mark asked me to stay after class. He had something to tell me which he had kept secret.

I had come to know him as a gifted poet and hard-working writer and speaker. Harder than most, perhaps, because Mark suffered from MS which had affected his coordination and vocal cords. Some days the class and I understood him better than others.

"Do you remember the first day of class when I refused to remove my hat?" he asked.

"Oh yes I do," I answered.

"Well, now I would like to tell you why I did that. About a year ago I went to an open mic forum to read my poetry. They laughed at me."

"They what?" I asked not wanting to believe what I was hearing.

"They laughed." His speech was labored and painfully slow. "I was humiliated."

Once again like that first day of class we were alone in my classroom. We looked at one another through our tears.

"The first day of this class when I refused to remove my hat I was trying to get you to throw me out of your class. The course was required but I did not want to ever stand before an audience again and perform my writing. But you would not give up on me. You would not let me leave."

"You chose to stay, Mark," I answered softly. We stood there for a moment looking at one another.

For his final persuasive speech, Mark spoke on Stem Cell Research Funding. He passionately argued for our government to acknowledge that it is his quality of life they are ignoring and for his classmates to vote for legislators who would make the stem cell reality happen. Would it be soon enough for him we all agonizingly wondered?

After offering an articulate and informed argument, with great difficulty Mark walked to his visual aid which was an empty white poster board. He asked his audience to give him one thing. Only one thing. He picked up a marker and with a shaking hand one letter painstakingly at a time he wrote, "Hope."

A year after he had completed my course, Mark came to my office to say hello. He proudly told me that students from our class would stop him in the hall and tell him that they would never forget his last speech. The MS was progressive and he was suffering. Yet he looked happy and at peace with himself. He had formed a team in his name for the MS Walk each year and was trying to raise money to help himself and others through funding for research.

Three years later I received an e-mail from him. He wanted me to know that he was writing again and that for the first time since he had been traumatized by the experience he again performed his poetry in an open mic at a Chicago club. He said he could have never done it without my course and my friendship. In his last line he told me that he always wore his cherished hat.

It was I who had learned a lesson from my student Mark. I had always been a professor who asked myself why a student acted in a certain way. I once thought the reasons for my students' behavior were something I could figure out through my insight and empathy. I now realized that the answers I needed to understand could be hidden under a hat.

Previously published in *"The Ultimate Teacher" and "Thin Threads"*

PERSPECTIVE
By Louise Borad Gerber

I

I feel sorry for Naomi
    so undemanding and complacent,
    unaware beyond her immediate sensations,
missing the color of celebrations and holidays,
dependent on others for her care.
    So often in isolation
whipping a piece of string or cloth for hours, or
watching her reflection in mirrors, or
    listening to records so often heard.
    She has words without meanings
    but no words to communicate feelings, and desires.
    Oblivious to her neediness, her shortcomings,
    to the sameness of her life,
    to her lack of growth, and to the growth of others.
I feel sorry for me
   still noticing how different Naomi is
      different than the daughter I expected.

II

How fortunate Naomi is
    not needing events, parties, friends or hoopla.
    She enjoys her world
        of songs and picture books,
          family and teachers.
   Satisfied with what is provided,
desiring no more than what she has.
    Carrying no scars from the past,
she lives in the present, without regrets.
    Her love of life shines from her eyes and smile.
How fortunate I am
    To have a daughter who has taught me lessons,
    about expectations and acceptance.

GRANDPA'S WORDS AND ACTIONS
By William Ricci

Rugged facial features and expressions, like that of mountain men in history books standing atop the highest peak and planting a flag for their country, shaped by endless sun and high arctic winds. He handled life and the people around him with the ease and care of a seasoned glassmaker. It was extremely difficult for me to believe that was my grandfather lying before me, thin, frail, a skeleton of his former self.

As a child four or five years old, my mother divorced and we moved into my grandparent's home, where she grew up on Main Street. Now after a few years, looking back on how life brought me to today, I believe this was fate. The moment afforded a chance for my mother and me to develop a bond, not only as parent and child, but with my grandparents. These bonds would stand time and distance, coming to fruition upon my grandfather's passing. Time has not softened the heart which still yearns to hear his voice and the raw, unpolished words.

On April 17th, I stood at the foot of grandfather's bed with him resting comfortably back home in St. Anthony. I did not know at the time that these were my last few remaining moments with him to talk, listen, and learn more of his life. For a man who would pass away the next day, he was his old and inquisitive self. His dark chocolate round eyes piercing through me were soft, but looking for something. Perhaps they were trying to find closure in the last hours. His face still had the character and unique features from years back when I helped him paint a brown wooden fence. I remember the backyard that always had the smell of baked breads, waffling from the kitchen where grandma was busy. A tall apple tree stood in the middle year after year, providing fruit and color. The tree reminds me of him: rigid, set in his ways, stubborn and able to withstand and overcome any challenge. Like the tree surviving a harsh winter, he had gone through many hardships and trials, with dignity and courage that stayed with him to the very end. Through his years, he did so many things, large and small, that have contributed to who I am as a person today.

While living on Main Street and adjusting to a new life with my grandparents and mother, I had an obsession with au gratin potatoes. They were the only sustenance I ever wanted; breakfast, lunch and dinner, whenever hunger pangs took over. If there was none to be found in the cupboards, grandfather would take my hand and with no questions asked, lead me out the front door, into the car and off to the local Snyder's on Central Ave. This kind of gesture was etched into my memory as his way of showing he loved me, without having to say the words.

Many children grew up with a blanket, providing security and comfort at the most stressful times. I was no different. Wrapping my arms firmly around the vivid colors of Winnie the Pooh and his friends, I clung to the blanket all the time. My fingers deeply entrenched, cotton and thread entwined with skin.

It was seven or eight in the evening while standing on the front porch, frightened, yet curious and fascinated by the flashing and noise. The night was alive with thunder clapping in the shrinking distance, flashes of light, the wind blowing hard through the trees, branches swaying. Caught off guard for a moment, a gust of wind rose from the east and ripped the blanket from my grasp.

My security was torn from me, my heart beating faster and faster, as though it would fly through my chest and into the wind. Looking into the direction I thought it flew, in between raindrops more fierce and heavy than minutes before into the void of the night, I kept the thought alive that it would come back and return to my open arms. It never did.

I was crushed and devastated; it left me screaming and crying, my eyes welling up at the slightest thought or mention of the blanket. I was vulnerable and searching for anything to deal with this moment. Fortunately, there was comfort to be found: Grandfather's kind and soothing words calmed me down, further cementing this man as a father figure. Although the loss could not be fixed or changed, he was there for me. His kind words and encouragement also helped in many other ways.

I often built things with Lego's, Constructs and Electra sets, typical toys of the early 1980s. These real-world things became reality as my imagination oozed into my fingers and assembled them, piece by piece: racecars with huge, spongy rubber tires and fast engines; cities of tall buildings and skyscrapers that reached for miles. Building these structures gave me a tremendous sense of accomplishment. Standing in awe and knowing that the images became something concrete and useful. The expression on my face conveyed these feelings: my eyes were bulging with excitement and I would be smiling from ear to ear.

When I would finish a project, I would take it to my grandfather and he would look it over. His words "This is really good, you should be an engineer" pushed me to keep building and make the next one even better than the last. Encouraging words from this man became my motivation and heightened my desire to build more and seek his approval.

Christmas is a time for family and the chance to see the loved ones from near and far. I cannot remember the gift I received from Grandma and Grandpa that year as there were more important memories to take away and energies to focus upon. I cherished this last time to see him as he always was: the man of pride, character and dignity. Christmas also brought with it a lot of questions I needed answers to: reasons why, the purpose that as a 17-year-old losing a part of me, could not comprehend and answer myself. How could this man of such strength and dignity be brought down by an illness, a life turned upside and spiraling so quickly?

In November of 1990, Grandpa was diagnosed with esophageal cancer. He had limited time left and we had limited time with him. Was I just losing a grandfather? It was much deeper and more profound than that. I was losing a friend, security, and someone deeply loved; who helped me to grow and become who I am today; a person close to my heart and soul, who loved with no questions asked and nothing expected in return. How could a God of passion and grace take away the very heart and soul of an individual? How can God leave people with a void that can never be replaced? How could He take away the person who always had an encouraging word that made me strive for more, reach for the top, fulfill my potential, and utilize the gifts that were given to me? This man, who raised me while Mom worked, was the essence of the early stages of my life, planting seeds and giving advice that burned into my consciousness.

He showed me how to care for others and love my family and work hard for what I desired out of life. I guess that is why his death hit me so hard and impacted the way I think and go from day to day. My thoughts are always in motion and his presence always alive and guiding. I must strive in the present with the few chances that I have and utilize all opportunities that I am given.

It has been over 18 years since Grandpa's passing, and not a day is without thoughts of him, or I come across a subtle reminder. I cannot forget the day when I last saw him and he looked into my eyes and tried to smile. I could see his pain and suffering coming to an end and finally becoming free. Some days when I am weakest and in need of help, I look towards the Heavens and thank God he is looking down upon me. A guardian angel is that spirit of consciousness that makes an agonizing decision a bit easier, or a hand that turns you away from death. Mine rose into Heaven on April 18th, 1991. My life, outlook, and place in humanity have only improved since that devastating day that has become a blessing.

In this regard, a death can be a blessing: another chance to grow. It's that knock on the door that takes an effort to answer, and seize the gift staring back at you.

TRINKETS
By Lottie Corley

Heaven took Mama in '84
We looked at each other and opened her door.
Trinkets of love throughout the years,
My sisters and I broke into tears.
Lockets of hair and baby barrettes
Among all the trinkets that she had kept.
Handmade jewelry for her birthday and bright colored cards
That we had made.

So much life for you to live,
So much love for you to give.
You don't get a Mother's Day,
Or the joy of watching our children play.
So many memories fill my mind.
So many memories in so little time.
So much love for you to give.
And oh what a life that you had lived.

A mother, a teacher, and so much more,
A guardian angel at our door.
Trinkets of love throughout the years
And showing us how to face our fears.
Good-bye mama we miss you so,
And it's just so hard to let you go.
Trinkets of love you kept through the years
And wiping away all of our tears.

MARTI'S JEWELS
By Charlotte Jones

My only sister, Marti, was twelve years older and I idolized her. She had emerald eyes, ruby-red hair, a gift for practical jokes and perfect pitch. She could play anything on the piano after hearing it only once. Even with the age difference, we were very close, starting when I was five and she used to sneak me out of bed at night to play cards, until we were well into adulthood, laughing over some zany joke. She had the kind of deep, throaty guffaw that rang throughout the neighborhood. The first jewel of wisdom she ever gave me was, "Grab for the gusto and then lie about your age!"

Even though I moved away after college, we talked nearly every week. So imagine my shock when the phone rang very early one morning and it was her husband, Bill. My heart leapt into my throat when he said she'd had a severe stroke and probably would not live for another day. I arranged the first flight out and got there in time to say goodbye. I will never know if, in her coma, she sensed my presence with her, but I like to believe she did. I held her hand as she died – I can still remember how quickly it grew cold.

The next few days were a blur. Arrangements had to be made, people notified, parents consoled. I knew I had to give the eulogy; no one else who could do it.

During that week, I met hundreds of her piano students. They came to say their last good-byes to the closed pine casket. They didn't ask, "How did Marti die?" Everyone assumed it was a skiing accident, or her automobile ran off the road on one of her frequent weekend trips from Albuquerque to Denver.

Instead they asked, "How old was she really?" She was famous for lying about her age and she had the looks to get away with it. When I told them she was 54, one woman responded, "That rascal! I thought she was 38!" Marti's laugh rang far beyond the grave.

As her husband and I sorted through her things, we ran across her driver's license. The birth date was off by eleven years and I'm sure she is still laughing over that one. How she arranged this feat, I'll never know.

One quiet piano student told me through her tears how much she adored Marti. She wasn't sure she could ever play the piano again, now that Marti was gone. Marti had taught her to escape from her troubled home life into music. The music was her sanctuary. This slight, blonde girl of 17 continued, "I do have one question, though. It's about 'The Box.'"

'The Box' was porcelain, with an Oriental design and a lid that Marti kept on the grand piano. It contained the fingernail clippings of any and all students who showed up for lessons with their nails too long. Magically, the box was always empty on recital day.

"Were our nail clippings really in the chocolate chip cookies like Marti said?" she asked me.

All I could say was, "Marti liked her cookies crunchy," and smile to myself that she'd played another joke and her students had fallen for it.

While I had yet to absorb the impact of my only sibling's death, stories from a joyous childhood flooded my mind. When I was five and she was 17, we played our own form of hide-and-go-seek. I used to hide under the bathroom vanity as she got ready for a date. She'd sing, "Charlotte, where are you?" And she taught me to reply, "I'm down here in Hell," much to our mother's dismay.

During college, she and her sorority sisters drove around on weekends, one of them in the trunk with a ketchup-covered arm hanging out, just to see if anyone would notice. I'm not sure they ever managed to get the attention of the police, but I'm pretty sure I know whose idea this was.

But the best was her howling at the moon. Perhaps it was growing up in New Mexico where the skies are clear at night and the wolves sometimes come down out of the mountains. Marti's howl could not be distinguished from the real thing and she taught me to howl almost as well. In fact, she taught me a lot of things – how to laugh at yourself, even in the face of adversity, how to follow your creative dreams, how to make people feel special.

I always have been unsure if I believed in an afterlife and if Heaven existed as I'd been taught in Sunday School. All I know is the week following her death, I never slept and in my exhaustion, I wondered how I would have the strength and composure to speak at the funeral. The night before, I was lying in bed, tears overflowing, when I heard her voice. "Char-baby," she said, using her pet name for me. "This is Mar-baby. I want you to know that I'm OK. Everything is going to be OK." A warm, calming wave washed over me and I was able to sleep. One last jewel from my sister to me.

When the dust settled after the funeral, I had time to grasp the meaning of losing her. I realized I had lost my best friend, the person who knew me better than anyone else. The person who, along with my parents, had always been there for me. I felt a void of loneliness, an emptiness that would prove hard to fill.

Then her husband did the most generous thing possible – he gave me all of her jewelry. Every day, every moment, I have something on that was hers. I wear Marti's jewels to honor her and feel close to her. Even though I have never lied about my age, each piece reminds me of all the jewels of wisdom and laughter my sister gave me for over 40 years. She reminds me to live every day to the fullest, as if it were my last.

TO A LOVED ONE
By Sharon Bourke

Your presence
When you were with me
Remains even now
Though you are gone.

Your look
Your readiness to respond
Your affirmation
Of my gestures
Words
Thoughts
Even before I expressed them
Are still here,

Unexpected validations
Encouragements
To keep going, keep being
Because of you.

MISS "H."
By Cherise Wyneken

Miss Hamburger, my English teacher at Acalanes Union High School in Lafayette, California, during the 1940's, was affectionately called, Miss "H" by her students. We girls loved her most for her role as leader of the extra curricular activity modern dance.

A lovely woman, with striking black hair and a lithe slender body, she taught us how to move ours gracefully, to hear stories and see movements in music, to create and choreograph. We gained self-confidence through her acceptance and encouragement as we performed before an audience at spring and fall concerts. Our appreciation of music grew as we danced to "Hungarian Rhapsody No. 2," "Go Down Moses," or Tchaikovsky's, "Sleeping Beauty Waltz." Dance brought aspects of our subconscious out from behind our ego masks and let them move and be exposed.

But it was in her English class that I learned the most valuable lesson she offered. "I'm going to read you an article on anti-Semitism," she said to the class one day. "Then I want you to write a paper discussing it." I had never heard that term before and didn't have a clue as to what it meant. The article spoke of Hitler's aggrandizement of blond, blue-eyed Aryans above other races, of pogroms, ghettos, and discrimination involving Jews. I had been brought up in a Christian setting, sent to Sunday school and studied Bible stories. To me the word *Jew* simply meant God's people in the Old Testament times. Why should they be treated badly?

That day, seated in a wooden desk in a small classroom, my eyes were opened to the horror of racism. My innocent world of family, friends, music, and dance was suddenly expanded to include sounds of suffering from people outside my little circle. I strongly defended the Jews in my essay.

Just as dance brought out my feelings, Miss "H"'s introduction to prejudice was a stepping stone to inclusiveness. Her lesson, assimilated at a formative age, helped me deal with relationships in creative ways. Ultimately, I gained an international family: an African-American son-in-law, a Mexican-American son-in-law, a Jewish daughter-in-law, and even an Episcopalian (I was brought up Lutheran). Miss "H" wove patterns of tolerance into my life, allowing me to celebrate and appreciate the variety in my expanding family.

DR. CHARLES LYNCH: A MEMOIR
By Dr. Milton Burnett, Ed.D., LICSW, LADC

This is about a school and about a group of teachers who made a difference in one person's life, but it is about one teacher in particular. He was not the only positive person there but he was the most important to me. It was my first college course. The experience was to open a whole new world to me, a much different one from the world I knew and had been living. It is this first educational experience that laid down a foundation for my quest for learning and the desire to change.

It was at Empire State College's Center for Labor Studies, part of the State University of New York, that I started my first college course in 1978 at the age of 39. The course was "Research Paper Workshop," a course to prepare us to hopefully write the college papers that were to follow. But above all the courses that were to follow it was this one that would give me the incentive to continue with my education until at the age of 55, I was awarded the Doctorate of Education. The person behind this who seemed larger than life to me and someone I wanted to model my future after was Dr. Charles Lynch.

Professor Lynch was an African American with a Ph.D in English literature from Columbia University. At this time I was 39 years old and only a few months out of a rehabilitation center for drugs and alcohol. I had had a 20-year love affair with the streets of New York City and its night life, along with its bars in the Bronx and Manhattan. My biggest obstacle was that I was lacking in most of the basic grammar skills as I had dropped out of school in the ninth grade. What I had learned was all but forgotten, and of course my thinking and reasoning skills were still not on solid ground. But what the hell, I had been doctoring my thinking with booze and pot for years. My self esteem was in the basement and I felt completely out of place sitting in this classroom, as I questioned if I was making a big mistake in starting college at this point in my life. But then I would ask myself, "Would any time be right?"

Dr Lynch was a very imposing figure, all 6' 4" of him. He seemed to be larger than life and that is how he remains in my memory today. His English was impeccable, his shirt and pants never seemed to lack a crease. His demeanor and presentation were always low key, and he never raised his voice. That first day in his class I felt totally intimidated by him intellectually. At first I would be anxious when I would talk to him; fearful that I would not meet his expectations. Twenty years of street life was not exactly great training for an English grammar class. But he would always put me at ease eventually. His first encouragement came with a two-page paper I wrote on a subject that has since escaped my mind. When he handed the paper back to me he called me aside and suggested that I keep a diary if I wished to write, as he felt that I had something others might not have that would eventually be formalized by my education.

The first major paper that would meet the course requirements was to be written on the subject of one's own experience in life. When I heard this I thought, "Boy, do I have a hundred experiences I wanted to put on paper." I can still remember vividly writing this paper at my kitchen table in my apartment in the Bronx. It was my first apartment after coming out of rehab; most of the years of my drinking life had been spent in rooming houses. The apartment was on 201st Street and Bainbridge Avenue, one of the better neighborhoods of the city. I had found the kitchen table near the service entrance by the superintendent's apartment; it had a Formica top which I scrubbed down with Clorox to make sure I killed all the germs. I felt "what a find at a needed time." I also had an old Smith-Corona typewriter that I had picked up in a pawn shop some place in Manhattan. I had bought an old MLA and APA handbook on formatting papers at Barnes and Noble on 14th Street; most of its meaning was lost to me. I had bought a package of onion skin paper which had light blue lines as margins that I felt look very impressive. I am sure that was not the required paper, but I was sure it would look impressive to Dr. Lynch. There was a tea kettle on the stove and a full ash tray on the table.

I was late starting the paper; I had procrastinated until the last minute out of fear that I was going to be unable to do it. Consequently I was frantically trying to complete the paper that was due to be handed in by the next day's class which started at six. I had so many questions as to the correctness of what I was doing and no where to find answers at that time of night. My AA friends would not be happy with me calling them at what was probably around 1:00 am and asking them questions not related to booze or a desire to drink. The only interruptions to the buzzing confusion in my head were the ever present cockroaches which were always scampering about; no amount of prevention seemed to obliterate them. Welcome to apartment house living in New York City.

I do not remember the exact topic of the paper at this point in time, but I knew I was most anxious to write on some facet of my street life and experiences. This was as much for a shock factor as it was to point out how interesting my life had been, and to obtain the attention I craved from Dr. Lynch. It was after 3:00 am before I finally finished typing the paper; of course there were several words that had been smudged by my attempts to correct the typos. Needless to say, my typing skills were not the best. By the time I was finished I was wide awake and could not wait to hand in the paper that coming evening. This paper written so long ago remained in my possession for years until I moved several years ago and it was somehow misplaced.

Dr. Lynch gave me a C- on that work that I spent most of the night compiling. It was not the grade that was the important thing to me, however, but the comments he wrote on it. He encouraged me to continue with my writing and that I had a special gift, and that others might have gone through the same experiences but would not have the ability or the desire to put it in writing.

One evening about 10 years ago, I called Dr. Lynch at his home in Brooklyn, New York. I was feeling very nostalgic about those days. I was not sure he would remember who I was but then the light of memory dawned on him. I told him I wanted to thank him for a wonderful educational experience and for giving me the desire and will to succeed. Both these seeds had been planted by him at a time when it meant so much to me and still does today at 71 years old. His response to my call was that he never realized how a person can impact another. Dr. Lynch was the first person in my life who saw potential in me, when for so many years I had been beaten down literally and mentally. Dr. Lynch enabled me to turn my life around and take a positive path; I will always be grateful for that.

This paper is being written as I sit at my desk in an emergency room where I work nights doing psychological examinations. I know that the foundation of my success started at Empire State College back in 1978 with Dr. Lynch.

THE PAINT BOX
By Helen R. Carson

When I was just a little girl
My mother gave me a tin box
I opened it with total awe
And found a rainbow living there!

Red, green, purple, pink, and blue
The world a glitter, within my reach
Twinkly stars, butterflies, and baby dolls,
My house, my dog, and family too.

I could paint them all and all I did
Imagination with no end
The talent of a four year old
As rich and varied as those colors.

Years passed. I was not Monet!
My friends became my paint.
Each a different shade and hue
Within reach the whole universe still.

Blue, my favorite, clear skies every day
Loyal and steady, heartfelt to all
Wry sense of humor, partner in crime
Lives in my soul forever, Sandy.

Red drama brings theater to my door
Dark, flashing eyes, beautiful Valentine girl
Who listens and laughs and cries
Class act, ageless Bobbie.

Green woodsy knoll, secret garden gate,
The most gracious hostess of them all
Lifelong scholar, with theory for everything
That beloved, elegant one, Bev.

Pink pearl chic, finest things of taste
Crystal edged, sterling silver trim,
Linen table, a bouquet of flowers
To brighten every day, Vivian.

Purple evokes deep passion and art
Delectable detail and design
Her laugh is infectious, a giggle divine
Her talent incredible, Janet.

The paint box of my life is full.
Rainbows of talent, wisdom and love
All wrapped up in five bright hues,
The girlfriends in my heart.

HE'S STILL HERE
Dedicated to my Sweet Daddy
By Dana Taylor

The old man stumbles, about to fall
To strangers he's barely a man, no one at all
Just a stick figure, bent and confused
Society's discard in the heap of refuse
His speech is garbled, a childish babble
One more elder in the crowd of old rabble

But look beyond the deterioration
Old bones once defended a nation
See in his eyes the trace of the soldier
The body is aged, but the spirit no older

Before the years of wife, children and work
He reported for duty he never would shirk
Marching from home at the outbreak of war
He traveled to lands never seen much before

A callow recruit full of bluster and youth
He fought for liberty, freedom and truth
The sights he saw brought shock and dismay
Burned into his memory day after day

A boy caught in battle, unsure and green
Transformed through war to a mighty Marine
Forever changed, forever the fighter
Now age is the enemy, it pulls the noose tighter

He faces life with a warrior's heart
Each day is a battle, right from the start
He won't give in to helpless despair
Won't use a cane or a smooth wheeling chair

His walk wobbles as he strolls round the block
His fierce independence comes as a shock
The old man knows death, struggle and fear
Look closely, you'll see, the Marine is still here

NEVER GIVE UP
By Lorraine Quirke

From the time I started high school, I dreamed of being a singer. I studied with teachers most of my adult life. Nerves and fear played a role in crushing my hope to sing professionally. I had talent, but talent isn't always enough. Stage fright ruined my performances and professional choruses wouldn't hire me because I couldn't sight-read. I tried to learn it by taking courses and practicing, but always failed in my auditions. Frustration and apprehension became my soul mates. I would ask myself, "Why did God give me a wonderful talent and not give the other tools to achieve it?" After years of failing, I became mad at myself and angry with God. Feeling miserable, I decided to give up my dream!

What do you do when your circumstances get tough? Do you give up or press on with God's help? Do you become miserable and blame God for your circumstances or do you look to Him for the answer? "Let us not become weary in doing good, for at the proper time we will reap a harvest if we do not give up." Galatians 6:9.

We can become tired but we must continue our path.

If we give our problems to the Lord instead of trying to figure them out ourselves, we become more trusting and less fearful because we know that God is in control of our lives. We know that whatever happens, it is God's plan at work for our greater good. Some events in our lives are painful and we question the outcome. However, He is the Supreme Being and knows everything. We have to rely on that no matter what we see, feel or believe to be true. Proverbs 3:5, says trust in the Lord and not to lean on our own understanding. "The steps of man are ordered by the Lord." Psalm 37:5.

My Aunt Gert has always had the motto *"Never Give Up."* She has overcome every problem because of her faith and trust in the Almighty. She convinced a depressed friend going through a divorce the Lord was walking beside her, holding her hand. Sometimes the Lord speaks through our friends with words of wisdom and a gentle touch. They talk every week and help each other through their problems.

Gert had confronted illness, death and financial problems with great courage and always came through them victorious. When she reached 99-years-old, many people admired her because of her determination to complete the course. Her doctors thought she was remarkable and wanted to know her secret for staying young and remaining healthy. She happily told them, "Determination not to give up, eating healthy, exercising and a positive outlook on life is the way to achieve longevity." I believe her indomitable spirit and giving nature are important too. The Lord has richly blessed her, and she is a shining example to all who know her. This reliance on Him is what brings her through the dark times–when the pain is unbearable. How did she acquire these qualities? They have come from hearing and believing the Word of God.

My aunt is reaping the benefits of what she has sowed all of her life. When her neighbor's children were young, she would always make sure that at Christmas they each had a toy and would give the family food and loving kindness. These children are now grown up and are reaching out to my aunt with the same compassion that she gave to them. Showing love and reaching out to others always comes back to you twofold.

She was like a second mother to me and as I was growing up I never lacked for toys and love. She would visit often and try to mediate problems that would arise between my mother, brother and me. Although she would become embroiled in our problems and get into trouble because of it, she never gave up trying to help us.

Being confident she puts herself in the hands of God and never worries about her problems to the point of becoming ill or depressed. She looks at every difficulty in a positive way. She once washed her kitchen floor and did other housework while in a wheelchair. It is this determination with a dependence on God that is the secret to a long and happy life.

My friend Ellen had the same determination. She worked all day and went to school in the evenings to get a degree. There were times she could feel defeat heading her way but she accomplished her goal in eight grueling years. Those eight years were difficult but the result was rewarding. Receiving a degree raised her self-esteem and gave her new opportunities in the job market. Was it worth it? She would say a resounding yes!

Kayaker Cliff Meidl, a two-time Olympian took part in the 2000 Olympics. His fellow participants named him flag-bearer at the opening ceremonies. What makes him so special is that years earlier he was accidentally electrocuted while using a jackhammer and absorbed 30,000 volts of electricity – 15 times the charge of the deadly electric chair. He did not die, but he had three cardiac arrests, and thought he would lose both his legs. Meidl's knees took the brunt of the shock, which also blew off toes and a portion of his skull, and burned a substantial portion of his back, where the voltage exited the body. He had many surgeries and with determination he walked again. He credits God with a miracle and feels blessed. He made a statement just recently that he hopes his story will encourage everyone to Never Give Up!

If we apply this determination and never give up attitude to our spiritual life we can be winners. With this strength of spirit and God's help we can achieve whatever the Lord asks of us. We can get through the problems, the fears and adversities of life. It is not always easy to be positive when life is beating us down but we can do it.

The Apostle Paul is the best example of someone with that attitude. He did the will of the Lord no matter the consequences. He raced for the prize and he never gave up. Paul said, "I have fought the good fight; I have finished the race; I have kept the faith."

Although most of us want to live a life pleasing to God, there are some attitudes such as complaining, depression, fear, and not wanting to wait for God's timing that can hinder our progress. When we fill our mind with negative thinking we develop the attitude "I can't do it."

My aunt went to be with the Lord two months before her 102nd birthday. The Lord blessed her with a long life because of her determination, blind faith and trust.

Taking all of this advice to heart, I have decided to change my attitude and get rid of that give up spirit and begin to live a life pleasing to God. Maybe I will sing for the Lord someday! I imagine that I will step out on a stage and my fear will disappear.

HE CALLED ME PRINCESS
By Susan Mahan

But he didn't mean one who
who wore a Royal family tiara
or one in a fairytale
with a fancy dress and a magic wand.

No.

What he meant was less obvious,
but more telling of our relationship.

When he called me Princess,
he could make the name sing with tenderness,
as if I were the only woman on the face of the earth.
Most times, for him, I think I was.
Most times, I needed to count on that.

He called me Princess with aplomb
if he wanted to defer to my judgment
or plaintively if he had reached the end of his rope
and wanted me to make the decision.
We trusted each other like that.

He called me Princess with an edge to his voice
if I was trying to get my own way,
and he thought I didn't deserve it.

He called me Princess in exasperation
when I wore him down in arguments
that could have gone either way.
I was really good at that.

He called me Princess with the barest hint of irony,
knowing full well that I did not lead
the life of a princess,
but that we are often
kidding ourselves in life, after all.
It's the way many of us get by.

Perspective colors everything.
We had one of our best laughs
when we learned that that this guy in work
had a dog named Princess.
Nice company I was keeping!

That Thursday night in the hospital,
with those raging leukemia cells poised
for what turned out to be the final blow,
his last words to me had been:

I love you, Princess.
You look tired. Go home and sleep.

Although I never said it to him in so many words,
I knew I had married a prince.

FOR ELENA MY SISTER IN ITZAPA, GUATEMALA
By Carolyn Ingram

When I close my eyes I hear the drum-beat
of tortillas slapped into form, the birds'
pio pio distant call. I see your aqua house
again, the first time I entered--our time
too short for holding back. Your shy sturdy beauty
tired from years shackled to work, watching
children without food. You fed sticks
into a wood burning stove, swept cement,
collected cold water to wash your clothes;
met with mothers, babies tied to their backs,
and pushed seeds into dirt; the small signs of success
surrounding you in circles--tiny fragrant pines,
ready to plant. When the mayor shut off the water--
without which you can neither wash nor cook
for Itzapa's children, or the volunteers
who work in the school born from your heart's calling,
the school you never attended, the hours you never played,
the hunger that kept your focus narrow
when you were so small--you protest. Elena I see
the bright blue and green coated shabby walls
of the room filled with splintered desks the government
school threw out. I see your children, taller
than you, dressed in corte and huipil;
your youngest in jeans; your granddaughter the first
with time to play. Elena, if I had been born
in your place, I wouldn't have been like you.
I might have been one to follow your lead.
If you had gone to school, I know you
could have been anything, yet no more than you already are.

WRESTLING WITH AN ANGEL
By Neil Whitman

wrestling with angels --
martial or spiritual
weakness into strength

Whether you think the *Bible* is a divine book, great literature or both, "wrestling with an angel" is a powerful image. Just as a reminder: in Genesis we see Jacob holding onto an angel to bless him before he confronts his brother, Esau, whom he wronged long ago. Haven't we all wrestled with angels? Here is one of mine.

Like many of you, I worked summers to earn money for college. Since age 14, I had worked in warehouses. But I wanted something different the summer of 1969 after graduating from the University of Massachusetts. I knew this would by my last so-called summer job of manual labor. Once I got to graduate school at the University of Michigan to study college administration, I knew that my department would find me work – university work.

Well, back in my hometown, Framingham, Massachusetts, I applied for a job at the local McDonalds and its manager, Mr. Ferguson, with a bit of a mocking tone, made me the "Big Mac Man" because, as he put it, I was a college GRAD-U-ATE.

I started on a Monday and Mr. Ferguson walked me through the seven steps to make a Big Mac. As he deliberately talked to me as if I were an idiot, I began to regret I was not back to loading trucks. By the end of the day, I had all the steps down pat and had no problem as, each of the following days I assembled my masterpieces one at a time.

Monday, Tuesday, Wednesday, Thursday, each day, all was well: Big Macs, one at a time, each a masterpiece. Then on Friday, I was on the night shift. Suddenly, as lines at the windows lengthened, I could not keep up. The assistant manager, a HIGH SCHOOL GRAD-U-ATE my age, kept yelling back at me: "Whitman, more Big Macs! Let's go. Move it."

Out of frustration, I yelled back: "But, I can't make 'em that fast."
Then Mr. Ferguson barked, "Yes, you can."
"But," I replied, "I don't know how!"
"Yes, you do. Figure it out."
And, by golly, I did. Suddenly a light went on.

"Oh, I see – a dozen at time; one dozen, each in one step of the production."

Soon, 84 Big Macs at a time were in production. Big Macs coming out of the wazoo!

The assistant manager had to call me off, "Whitman, hold it. Take a break, enough of the Big Macs."

I looked at Mr. Ferguson and he gave me a big wink. I knew it would be a good summer.

And, I learned a lesson that did not make it into the college administration curriculum at Michigan. *Do not give adults information in advance of their need for it.*

Thank you, Mr. Ferguson for pinning me down.

RANDOM ACTS OF KINDNESS
By Carolyn T. Johnson

The overall mood at the Charity Pasta Party was somber. The patrons glanced at expensive auction items, picked up pens to write bid numbers then returned the pens unused. Even the lavish buffet, in all its splendor, was barely touched. Only the bartenders saw a steady stream of customers.

Not seeing a familiar face in the small crowd, I nibbled on a few hors d'oeuvres, ordered a glass of wine and wandered over to the auction tables. People were browsing but few were bidding and those who were bidding were only offering the minimum.

A placard with a picture of an elegant, refined lady striking a casual pose caught my eye. The caption read, "Lunch with NY Times Best Selling Author, Judith McNaught". I was drawn to read the fine print. She was a well-known romance writer who lived in town and was offering to have lunch with the lucky winner and present their manuscript to her editor for review.

I didn't have three words written on the same page much less a manuscript to present but I'd always wanted to be a writer, to get the stories out of my head and onto paper. Maybe this was just what I needed to get me started. I placed my bid.

When the auction closed, I was secretly happy no one outbid me and rushed to claim my prize. I presented my receipt to the table monitor when a lady wearing a beautiful, sparkling, full-length, seafoam-green gown extended her graceful hand in greeting. It was the author from the photo, Judith Mc Naught. She wanted to shake *my* hand – a real, live, successful author. Star-struck, I pumped her hand excitedly while telling her how thrilled I was to have won. She deftly extricated her hand from my grasp and graciously listened to me chatter on and on about wanting to be a writer.

I acted as if I was onstage accepting my first Academy Award, while she waited me out, her eyes twinkling. When I finally paused to take a breath, she smiled like an indulgent mentor. We visited a few minutes and then she gave me her card, said she was looking forward to our lunch and invited me to her house beforehand if I was interested.

Over a year later, still with no manuscript in hand, I rang the bell. She met me at the door in a white cowl-neck sweater and black slacks. Her home was what romantic novels are made of, lots of fluffy white furniture atop creamy white carpet with beautiful pieces of Baccarat crystal scattered about. Her study, overlooking the lake, had ceiling-high bookshelves lined with her best-sellers as well as other authors she knew. She even let me see her bedroom, which had at least 15 decorative pillows arranged across a plush, velvet bedcover. A small, crystal chandelier hung over her marble-clad bathtub. She smiled, "It's not a very practical bathtub, but it looks pretty."

She drove us to the seafood restaurant in her Mercedes two-seater she called "Baby Girl" while making small talk, so I would feel comfortable.

"Would you like to share a bottle of wine?" she asked. I nodded yes and the waiter disappeared. "You know I must have really liked you at the party because I was surprised when you reminded me I had invited you over to my home. I never do things like that."

I admitted that I was surprised too because I thought I had made a complete fool of myself babbling on like I did that night I met her. We both laughed.

"So, what would you like to know about writing?" she smiled, clasping her long manicured fingers daintily under her chin.

"How did you get started?" I asked.

She began her career by submitting her first novel, *Whitney My Love,* to editor after editor. They kept telling her to shorten it because no one was going to read a romance novel that long. Every time she got that response, she added a chapter until she finally found an editor who agreed to publish her novel in its entirety. That was her first best-seller.

I liked this lady. She was down-to-earth, sincere and persistent. In fact, she was a lot like me except I was a banker not a best-selling author. I admitted, "I have a decent vocabulary and my stories are always entertaining but I don't know if I can write."

"Don't let anyone tell you that you can't write just because you're in the finance field," she said. "You can be both creative and good with numbers. Let me show you what I mean. Clasp your fingers together and cross your thumbs. See how your right thumb is overlapping your left one? That means you are analytical. Now look when I do it." I was surprised to see her right thumb overlapping her left one too. "If you're creative, your left thumb is supposed to be on top," she grinned.

She even told me about the time she encountered writer's block and flew in a well-known guy from New York to help her. She admitted, in hindsight, it would have been just as helpful to buy his tapes and recommended I do so. She even gave me his number and said to tell him she told me to call.

We settled into familiar "girl talk." She told me about losing her husband just when her books started to sell, how she meets three of her girlfriends once a month for happy hour and how she hates car trouble.

We talked like old friends until it was time for "Baby Girl" to take us back and for me to go home. I felt a little silly asking her to sign her latest novel for me. She giggled, whipped it open to the title page and wrote, "To Carolyn, I had a wonderful time at lunch! Good luck with *your* book, Judith Mc Naught."

And now for the inscription on the title page of my successful transition from banker to writer, "Judith, you will never know the affect you have had on me. Your kind words *encouraged me, pushed me, inspired me* to become a published writer. Although I have not made my debut on the New York Times Best Seller list yet, that day may come because of you."

ANAFGHAT'S STORY
By Ann Reisfeld Boutté

On Monday, June 13, 2005, a headline on the front page of *The Wall Street Journal* caught my attention. It read, "Married at 11, A Teen in Niger Returns to School." Beneath the letters was a drawing of a delicate, young girl with dark eyes and long hair parted in the center and draped with a scarf.

The story introduced me to Anafghat Ayouba, no more than 15, a native Nigerian who was sitting on a stained hospital mattress. Married before her teens and pregnant after the onset of puberty, Anafghat was recovering from surgery to repair a fistula, a three-inch-wide hole in the bottom of her bladder caused by four days of labor.

It's a condition that afflicts more than one million young women in the so-called "fistula belt" along a southern stretch of the Sahara. Because of extreme poverty and religious and social customs, Nigerian preteen girls are often given by their families in marriage in exchange for a dowry. The girls become pregnant, but their bodies have not developed sufficiently to give birth. The prolonged labor ends in bladder damage.

Because of their incontinence and odor, many are ostracized by their families and forced to live by themselves or with each other. They may wait years for a team of visiting American doctors who pay their own expenses and donate their services, the only hope for the "lepers of the desert."

Anafghat was given in marriage for one camel. After nine months of pregnancy, she spent three days in labor before her family realized that she needed help. She was then taken more than 60 miles over rutted dirt roads to a hospital where she delivered a baby boy who was stillborn.

When I finished Anafghat's story, I sat for a long time at my kitchen table, thinking, reflecting, reduced to tears of sympathy, and humbled by my own circumstances. I sleep at night and spend my days free of pain. How foolish to spend one moment wishing for a prettier face, a better figure, or a wrinkle cure.

I live in a comfortable home amid items I've collected that bring me pleasant sensations and memories. I have enough space to close a door if I crave privacy or open it when I want the sounds of family. How petty to waste a minute envying those with more expensive homes and finer ornaments.

What folly to feel slighted by someone's inattention when I have real friends.

Shame on me for becoming annoyed with my husband over trivial matters when he is a kind and generous companion who makes me laugh.

As for my sons, I can only say that had I ordered them to specifications I would not have listed all the attributes they possess. It would have seemed too much to ask.

I do not discuss my connection with Anafghat. I consider it to be spiritual, and I do not want random comments to taint her lessons. I keep her story on a shelf in my closet where I can consult it if I want or need to.

In the newspaper account, Anafghat says that despite her early hardships, she has not lost her dreams and ambitions. When she recovers from surgery, she wants to return to the third grade which she was forced to leave when she married. She wants to go on to high school and college and become a doctor so that she can make a difference. I would tell her that she already has.

THE DAY MY UNCLE HANK SAT DOWN TO LUNCH WITH HELEN KELLER IN A CAFÉ IN THE PHILIPPINES, AUGUST 1948
By Paul Hostovsky

it was raining,
but raining so hard that he couldn't
see what his hands were doing
in front of his own face, so he climbed
carefully down from the truss
of the cantilever bridge he was building
with the Army Corps of Engineers outside
Manila, and made his way into the city under
friends' umbrellas twirling toward
the brothels mostly, but Uncle Hank
who was always more hungry than horny
headed for Fagayan's for a bowl of beef stew.

Helen was building bridges too, she told him —
"bridges out of Braille dots" (visiting schools
for the blind all over Asia). Then she smiled
and turned to Polly Thomson sitting beside her
(Annie Sullivan dead 10 years already)
and asked her if the young American soldier
sharing their table in the crowded café
with its red-and-white checkered tablecloths,
sounds of Tagalog, Spanish, English mixed
with the clacking curtain of rain filling the doorway —
was smiling at her Braille joke. Yes, he was,

but he couldn't see what her hand was doing —
the fitfully pecking bird of Polly's hand
finger-spelling into Helen's palm — to make
the words, *his* words, almost as fast as he was saying them:
"How do you do that, that, with your hand…how
does she understand?" And so it happened
that my mother's youngest brother Henry Weiss,
who hadn't written home in over six
months, learned the American Manual

Alphabet from its most famous reader,
over beef stew, brown bread and beer,
on a rainy day in Manila, and now had something

to write home about. Of course he'd heard
of Helen Keller — who hadn't? — but here
she was, older, stouter, and drinking
a beer, and sitting across from him, holding
his hand now, molding it, arranging his
fingers and thumb into the shapes of the letters
one by one, teaching him her tactile
ABCs. And her hands were large and strong
for a woman's hands, and she smelled good too,
and to see his eyes smiling when he told it
to my mother, whose eyes smiled telling it
to me years after, the way her generous
bosom swelled above the checkered table cloth
as she leaned in close to Uncle Hank
and shaped and sculpted and praised,

it aroused in him something he never quite
got over. And walking back to the barracks
in the pouring rain, gazing down at his right
hand still practicing the letters, feeding them
to his left, which he cupped like a nest under them,
he must have looked to anyone observing him
like a man bent over his own praying hands;
or a man wringing his hands, for love; or maybe
a man who has just found something small
and glinting, and of great value on the way
to wherever it was he was going, and pausing
in the middle of the road now, he considers
this strange, new, marvelous light it casts
on his hands, on the road, on his whole life.

THE ART OF BEING A GRANDMOTHER
By Joanne Seltzer

During my childhood in Detroit, old age seemed the magical time of a woman's life—a time for retrospection or for influencing history.

My mother's mother was the storyteller. At least once a week I visited Grandma, always hoping she would repeat some of her bittersweet memories: a baby's death, a daughter's marriage, the armistice that brought her sons home from the trenches of World War I. Born in Poland in 1861, Grandma grew up in Boston and was indelibly touched by the feminist movement of the middle to late 19th Century. The mother of ten, she never turned motherhood into a career. While Grandpa, an Orthodox Jew, was busy praying, studying Torah, or doing charitable works, Grandma minded the family store. She insisted that her four daughters graduate from teachers' college in an age when a high school diploma, especially for a woman, meant more than a Master's Degree today. As for marriage, Grandma told me what she had told her daughters: a woman with a profession has no need for a husband. Hardly a stereotyped meek old lady, Grandma owned rental houses and held bank accounts in her own name. She, not Grandpa, read the financial section of *The Detroit News*. She was the only family member who hated FDR.

My father's mother was the one who influenced history. *Mutter*, as everyone called her, came to America from Lithuania already a mature woman with husband and five children. Some 20 years later, in the early 1930's, she decided to relocate to Jerusalem. Her children, concerned about the hard life she would face in that legendary place called Palestine, begged her to abandon her visionary plans. But *Mutter*, a sixtyish widow, broken-hearted over the car accident that killed her lastborn child, my father, left for the Promised Land. Her letters to Detroit, written in Yiddish, told of one Jewish family that needed food, another that needed clothing, and another that needed a daughter's dowry. The American branch of our family sent money and hand-me-downs at least once a month, hoping *Mutter* would keep enough cash for her own modest needs.

During the 1948-1949 War of Independence, she dodged bullets and crawled through the rubble of bombed buildings in search of her adopted families. The sight of my grandmother making her daily rounds gave heart to other Jews: if this determined old woman, undaunted by war, still brought food to the hungry, how could anyone give up the fight? *Mutter*'s determination helped establish the Jewish State.

Now it's my turn to interpret the role of grandmother. Seventy-something seems not so decrepit anymore as I, Grandma Joanne, experience the magic my grandmothers lived. I've fallen in love with world travel of late but also enjoy staying home and cultivating my personality.

GRANDMA ESTHER
By Laurie Lee Didesch

You lived red, the color of flushed cheeks after chasing up a hill,
at the top smiling and heady at your accomplishment.
I imagine you might have done this in your childhood.
In my youth, you brought me a Mandarin doll from China Town
in silk and carrying a lantern like the sultry sun over the Bay
and a straw purse from Nassau stitched with fingers of yarn,
rays of the same brilliant star.

You traveled beyond widowhood and met a former Navy diver
who made you his poster girl. We called him Bernie.
A favorite photo rings with laughter: the one where
the grandkids piled on his lap, almost tipping an easy chair.
And when bells rang in the New Year, you and Bernie
chased us out of bed with hats and horns and noisemakers
we screeched along with as we twirled their handles.

All this, you must be telling Grandpa Lou, after so many years
apart. I know his soft chocolate eyes from your dresser top,
and how as newlyweds, he held you on the beach through
the hottest summer nights, a breeze off the lake and sand
skimming your legs. We buried those legs in red slacks.
Now, I keep a pair of your well-worn sandals, and they remind
me to keep after my own soles.

THE LITTLEST AMBASSADOR
By Lucille Joyner

It was night and I had to make that dreaded first-time trip to Newark International Airport to pick up my daughter. She asked that I bring ChiChi, her little Teacup Chihuahua that was in my care for the week. This added to my anxiety of driving at night.

The first thing that went wrong was that I barely missed an Irish Setter that had run out in front of my car. ChiChi was so frightened by my screeching brakes, she would not leave my arms. Trying to comfort a shivering puppy and being shaken up, myself, I missed my exit and found myself on Route 21. I was lost and pictured my daughter waiting restlessly at the terminal. My stress level rose to a piercing headache. I had no idea where Route 21 would take me, but at least I was going south. To my utter surprise, the gas station attendant said it went directly to the airport. My headache began to let up.

At arrivals, cars were being waved away by tired and frustrated police officers sporting long, ultra bright flashlights that I am sure doubled as weapons. I didn't see my daughter anywhere. I didn't know what to do next or where to go, so I beckoned a policewoman for help. She beckoned back at me as if to say, "You want me? You come to me!" If there ever was a hostile and belligerent attitude, hers was it, but I was too exhausted from the strain of night driving to even be angry or defensive.

I drove slowly up to her and rolled down the passenger window. She leaned forward with a look that told me I didn't have long to live. I had the feeling that this woman ate nails for breakfast.

Just as she was about to read me my last rites, she was distracted by the sight of ChiChi, who had rushed to the window and stretched her tiny body up to her. While there was no change in the officer's expression, she stood there staring in the face of a dog the size of a squirrel, that looked like a shrunken Doberman, with giant ears that looked like satellite dishes stuck on her walnut size head, poppy eyes as if she had a thyroid condition, and a face that looked like a Halloween mask.

The police officer did the unthinkable. Without a word – or a smile, for that matter – she slipped her hand into the car and began stroking the funny-faced little creature. ChiChi loved every moment of it and just looked up at her adoringly.

While she was petting ChiChi, my cell phone rang, and I'm sure the officer heard me reply, "You're still in customs?" I asked the officer how long I could park there, and without looking up she snapped, "For as long as I am petting this dog!" I felt like saying, "In that case, keep on petting," but I wasn't sure that behind that stony face was a sense of humor, so I kept silent.

She stroke ChiChi tenderly for at least five minutes, which is a very long time when cars, taxis, and limos are piling up all around. It was as though she needed this tender moment to escape from the pressures of her grueling job. Spellbound by this connection with ChiChi, her universe disappeared, and all that was left was her and ChiChi. She did not want to leave.

Finally, she had to break away to help her struggling partner, who was commandeering the traffic overload alone. She stopped petting abruptly and as she walked away, she waved her hand toward the center of the arrivals curb and barked, "You can pull in over there!"

As I was headed toward that space, her partner lunged in my direction menacingly, shining his huge powerful flashlight in my eyes from around 20 feet away. He took a few hard steps in my direction, ready to nail me, when the policewoman saw him. I don't know what she shouted, but whatever it was, he did a 90 degree turn and switched the beam to another driver. She then pointed to a clear spot up ahead, away from the traffic jam, where my presence would not hamper their work, and I was allowed to park there for as long as I needed.

In my rear view mirror, I could see that drivers were not allowed to park or stop for more than a few minutes. Even when their party was there, they had only a minute to throw the bags into the car and take off. You couldn't get away with a thing under the watchful eye of the police officers. They knew what was going on every minute with every car. To avoid a ticket, you were forced to circle the airport until you got lucky and your party was there. I saw no exceptions.

I sat there in my privileged parking space, relieved but stunned. The policewoman had not softened towards me, or at least seemed not to by all external appearances, but something had definitely happened. I concluded that unconditional love, even from a peculiarly cartoon-like little puppy, had the magical power to soften the heart of a tough Newark Airport policewoman.

THE TOUGH PART OF EASY
By Lucy Jubilee Barnett

I was a bright child who loved to read which should have made me an enthusiastic student. While I often had excellent grades, there was little joy and even less work. The children that struggled with schoolwork often found it easy to quit, but my natural strengths made it hard for me to get started. Whether I was painted as lazy or unmotivated, the end result was very little completed schoolwork. I knew that no matter what I didn't do, I would still have a report card decorated with a glinting string of A's.

Mr. Graham entered my life in Grade Six and I knew his reputation around the school as tough but fun. I can still remember sitting in his class on a hot September day as he introduced himself and made it clear what he expected from us. He was the first teacher I had who deviated from the lesson plans and tried to tailor curriculum to match the student's levels. He had a dry sense of humor, a firm hand and was a big believer in personal responsibility. In other words, to a bunch of sixth graders, he towered over us in estimation and was as refreshing as he was frightening.

For me, everything had changed but I was still the same. I was more connected to school and felt a greater sense of challenge from Mr. Graham but I was still able to pick and choose what I wanted to do. I was so used to looking at success in school as being the sum of my grades; I didn't understand that there were other ways of measuring progress.

As I got to know Mr. Graham better, I learned that there was more than one way of maintaining respect and control in the classroom. Previously, there had always been calls to simmer-down or consequences like writing lines as a boring but ineffectual punishment. Mr. Graham managed even the toughest kids with a long, measured look or a quiet word at recess. He was so likeable that we all craved his respect even though we were unlikely to admit it.

It was a Thursday morning and the Wednesday evening should have been spent working through a series of math questions. I had the graph paper, the pencil and the time. I just had lacked the motivation. When my lack of homework was combined with my daydreaming in class, the result was that I was completely unprepared when Mr.

Graham called my name. Prior to that point, I had been staring down at the pitted top of my desk, hoping not to be called on.

"Lucy, what is the answer to question 18?" Mr. Graham addressed me with a pointed look. It was unusual for me not to volunteer an answer in class.

"I don't know." I tried to be casual but I felt really embarrassed having to admit it.

"Did you complete the homework from last night?" I wanted to be honest, if nothing else.

"No." I could have heard a pin drop if my heart wasn't pounding out from my ears.

Mr. Graham's gaze was level with mine.

"I'm very disappointed in you." Without waiting for a response, he carried on taking up the homework. He didn't rub it on or rake me over the coals but Mr. Graham was effective. I felt ashamed that I had let him down but even more conscious that I had let myself down. Mr. Graham never mentioned it again and from then on, it was rare that I didn't finish my homework.

He had taught me that doing what is expected shouldn't be motivated by impressing others or external measures of excellence. Often, it is connected to personal integrity and the knowledge that the best measures of education are internal and never seen. By avoiding my responsibilities, I was not just disrespecting Mr. Graham; I was doing myself a disservice and courting avoidance rather than discipline. When measured with enthusiasm and patience, discipline is the backbone of every new skill. Mr. Graham taught me that while many things would come easier to me, complacency would limit my options and managed control would help me to excel at anything.

He probably never knew the impact of those five words but Mr. Graham's sentence has helped to guide me from then to now. Mixing the tough with the easy has made me reach for new challenges every day and know that I have the drive to make anything work. At the end of the day, he taught me that true learning is not built from a system of letters but is born from the warm glow of self respect.

EXPOSE YOUR FOIBLES
By Melanie Rigney

"I want you all to unzip your souls and expose your foibles," the writers' conference speaker, Patricia Lorenz, said. "People don't want to read about people who are perfect. They want to read about people who mess up!"

"Look at me—I've been divorced twice, and my second husband left me for an older woman!" she continued with a laugh. "For 20 straight years, I put four kids through college on a freelance writer's income! And I've had 20 different men sleeping in my house in the past ten years."

Patricia waited for all of our jaws to hit the floor before she explained that pilots stayed in her home occasionally because she lived so close to the Milwaukee airport.

I sat in stunned silence. Did this woman have no filters, no need for privacy? I knew I'd never share with anyone my late father's alcoholism and mental illness, my fear that any day now someone was going to figure out I was a total fraud of an editor, my nagging concern about my marriage's financial situation. What good would writing any of that do? And I certainly wasn't going to talk about my problems in front of total strangers. After all, I spoke regularly at writers' conferences across the country on topics such as self-publishing, novel writing, essay writing, and marketing your work. I surely couldn't let attendees see how truly alone and vulnerable I felt.

"Unzip your soul and expose your foibles," Patricia said that day in 2002. Several years have passed, and I now believe that's exactly what God wants us to do. I believe he wants us to come to him just the way we are. And, I believe in the life-transforming power of friendship. Patricia, who's been my dearest friend for the past eight years, and eleven other people inspired me enough with the way they live their faith that I returned to Catholicism and God after more than 30 years in the desert. She and others stood by me as I left my husband to begin life in a new city with a new job. They kept me going as I navigated the painful experience of divorce and of repaying more than $100,000 in credit card debt in just three years. They celebrated with me as I began a new life, richer spiritually, emotionally, and financially.

And, they all helped me to understand that God loves me just as I am, foibles and all.

POETRY IN MOTION
By Eve Hall

Sometimes we find things when we least expect them. That's what happened

to me. "Seek and ye shall find," that's what the good book says. I was not

looking for this particular 'thing' that I found. Let me explain.

I am a published writer and poet, with poetry being my first love.

I have poetry on the brain. I wake up thinking about it and it is the last thing

I think about before I retire at night. In my spare time, which I am having

less and less of these days, I surf the online poetry sites.

As I was surfing the poetry websites, I came across a poem that touched my

heart and soul. I wrote the author and expressed how I felt about the poem.

The way the author spelled their name, I was looking forward to a female poet's reply.

When I received the reply, I was a bit surprised, if not shocked to find out it was a male

I figured this poem was just a fluke, so I went over to the site to read more of his work.

I enjoyed reading his work. I will call my friend,
LB. Although, our backgrounds are

different, racially, socially and spiritually, we get
along fine, NOW. We did not get along

at all, in the beginning. You see, LB, is a
recovering cocaine addict. There were times

when I thought it was not worth it to keep
writing him, but I continued to write him and

he would always answer right back. I had let
him know I had just finished reading the

entire Bible. He was impressed but, at the same
time, a little cynical about me believing

everything I read. He also told me about his
wife's views on people that were not,

'White.' She felt that anyone who was of a
different color was inferior.

I had to let him know right then that the woman
he was writing, was smart and Black!

He was a bit surprised, but not daunted in the
least.

LB's father passed away during our
correspondence. His dad had been confined to a

wheelchair, and LB chose to take care of him. I
always told LB to tell his father how

much he loved him. LB now finds more time to
ride his motorcycle. Yes, he is a biker.

Our friendship has truly grown since it started
over six years ago.

LB, respects me as a woman, poet and friend
My favorite poem is by, Maya Angelou

entitled, 'Phenomenal Woman.' This is what he thinks I am. I think he is a, 'Phenomenal

Man.' I will have to get LB's consent to have this story published so if you are

reading this story you know he gave me permission to have it published

LB, may be a recovering cocaine addict, but he is also my, 'addiction.'

BECOMING NOBODY
By Rebekah Crain

As I walk to my building, several soldiers salute me. I return their salute with the usual greeting. I enter my office, greet my soldiers and begin working on the training schedule, coordinating my plans with my commander's plans. He calls a key leaders meeting; we're briefed on the situation in Iraq. Because I know the equipment I will go first to set up the site if we get called up. We run through field exercises and drills to keep our equipment ready and our skills sharp. My crews are green and my bags are packed. I am ready to go.

That was a long time ago, before the accident that changed everything, making me wonder who I am and where I fit. I was hit by a car while I was training for a race; I recovered, but it left permanent brain damage. I tried to make it on my own but was diagnosed with yet another problem, so I moved from California to Oklahoma feeling dejected, confused and wounded. I was somebody: I used to be an officer in the United States military, and then I was just nobody wandering the streets daily looking for work.

I relocated Oklahoma because my mother lived there and she could watch my daughter while I looked for work and went back to school. I hoped going to school would make me more marketable despite my impairments and lack of experience outside of the military. However I was not optimistic. I tried to internalize the emotions so I would not bring the people around me down too, but it was hard to keep my story from spilling out of my mouth in conversations with new acquaintances. I knew what I had lost and I felt it every day; it was as if I was living in a sort of shock.

To make ends meet I finally found a job as a social worker. My salary was roughly half of what it had been before the accident. I told myself not to complain, a job was better than no job and besides, I was helping people, but it was hard to listen to that rational voice. I still wanted to be more. When I started work I watched the other workers, some were bitter and cynical while others believed they were making a difference in the lives of their clients. By some workers I was warned to never trust clients and to look for the inconsistencies in their stories, and by others to remember the clients were people, therefore I should be consistent and fair in dealing with them. In my coworkers I saw patience as they got screamed at by clients who did not meet guidelines, kindness as they comforted those who had nowhere else to go and who were under duress.

When I finally got to work with my own clients, my eyes were opened. I have never been rich, but I was amazed at the conditions I saw on some home visits: apartments where none of the appliances worked and carpets were matted with dirt, or toilets piled with feces because property management couldn't get out to take care of the problem. On that visit the child told me she had wash-downs with a washcloth in the kitchen sink; my heart broke for her innocence. As I looked at income statements, I wondered how people made it on so little. This is America and some clients were living on $300 a month, which would be roughly $3,600 annually. In some Third World countries, a middle-class income is $3,000 a year; I wondered as I made that comparison were these people rich compared to the world or poor because they lived in America. I still don't have that answer.

Other clients came in after months of being laid off because they had exhausted all other resources and we were the last stop as they continued to search for another job. I saw one of my pregnant clients walk a quarter mile beyond her bus stop to get to class because that was the closest the bus could get her. She complained to me about dodging loose dogs on her walk between the bus and the school; she wanted advice about getting them out of there. I had an angry homeless vet, who was living in her car, yell at me because it was against our office policy for me to give her money for gas. "This is just a job to you," she screamed. "You don't really give a damn about anyone." She stormed out of the interview room.

In my interviews I saw frustration, angst and sadness. Some clients told me I could never understand their situation, they thought I had everything. I wanted to hug them, explain that I understood more than they knew. They didn't know what I had been through or that my accident had made me dependent on others for rides; I had to ride the bus occasionally just like them. I was softening; I had a job to do and guidelines to follow, but I saw stories and people in that office. People struggling to make it through each day and searching for their place in this world just like me.

There are days where I remember life before my accident and what I used to be with a nostalgic fondness, but I am prouder of who I am growing into as I approach the world with wide open eyes looking for people who are lost, lonely or sad, ready to help them. I have finished school now, but I'm still nobody and I'm okay with that. I enjoy swimming in the sea of nobodies where we all share a part of the same story.

LOVE LEARNED
By Tina Traster

Everyone said I'd fall in love the minute they laid her in my arms. She was beautiful – a broad alabaster face with slightly-slanted deep brown eyes. She was a flirt: at 6 months she knew how to flash a dimpled smile, like a come-hither starlet. I was awed by her perfect features as the fleshy woman pressed her into my arms, swaddled in a blanket. A few minutes later she said, "Feed baby," and handed me a bottle filled with a brown tea concoction. I took the bottle hesitantly and tipped it toward the baby's pursed lips. How would I know when she was sated or whether she needed to burp? I felt as though someone had lent me an expensive camera I was afraid to fiddle with.

At the airport waiting to leave Siberia I had our baby on my lap. Suddenly I heard a pop, then a mountainous ooze of putrid yellow diarrhea exploded from her diaper. I was horrified, unable to stand the smell of the stench. I thrust the baby into my husband's hands. Calmly he changed her diaper and pulled out a clean snowsuit.

Terrified my first instinct was to push this baby away from me rather than come to her aid; I wondered how in the world I would be able to care for her. I was 40 when we went to Russia, in a second marriage, one I trusted would last. Becoming a parent was the next thing to do, like ticking a chore off an errand list. My husband and I had tried basic, non-invasive fertility treatment because we couldn't conceive; when that failed we moved on to adoption without any real aching over the lost hope of having a genetic child. I was secretly relieved because I didn't want to expose my body to more aggressive, hormone-altering fertility treatment like in vitro fertilization. Maybe I felt ambivalent about motherhood and didn't know it.

Never did I sit myself down and think, I mean really think, about how I felt about motherhood. Six months after the social worker from the adoption agency called and said, "We have a baby for you," our daughter was in a makeshift nursery carved from a windowless alcove in our small apartment in New York City. There were no mobiles dangling above her crib or animal-themed borders running along the wall. We'd had just enough time to assemble a borrowed crib, an IKEA bureau of drawers and a changing table. The space was so teeny we couldn't even fit a rocking chair.

No one had thrown me a baby shower. I had not read a single book on preparing for parenthood. In the months leading up to the adoption, my husband lost his job. At times I wondered whether we should go through with it, but he convinced me we should. "We're both 40," he had said. "There's a baby who needs parents." I remember the steel-grey November day I got the call from the agency. I heard "Siberia" and "passports" and "arrange flight," but all I could think about were my writing deadlines.

Pregnant women get to arrange the spice rack. Nature slows them down. They come to their baby slowly, symbiotically. When we first brought the baby home she weighed 15 pounds. I had long-term neck and back injuries from sports so I could barely carry her. Putting her in a snuggly was out of the question.

During the first year I fed her and changed her diapers and sang to her before putting her in the crib, but I could just have easily been loading a dishwasher, paying bills. I was numb. I wasn't suffering from sleep deprivation because life at the orphanage had taught the baby to sleep 11 hours a night in a bed by herself. But I had not had a chance to welcome the mother in me. I had not mentally prepared for time to slow down – to be so needed.

I didn't believe I had the right to use the term "postpartum" depression but I was as blue as I'd ever been. I'd look down at my gorgeous child sitting on the floor with her little feet out in front of her, surrounded by blocks and other toys, and feel a surge of guilt.

At Mommy and Me groups other babies sat dutifully in mommy's lap. Every time we got to one of these classes my baby's first instinct was to bolt around the room, even when she was still crawling. I'd smile wanly at the neighboring mommy and say, "Oh, my little astronaut." Inside, I was screaming with rejection from this child.

I had gone to the end of the world to get this baby, yet we were not bonded.

I began to think I was damaged goods. Or she was. Perhaps I was not bonding to her because she was not bonding to me. There is a syndrome suffered by many adopted children where they do not attach to their new mothers and fathers. Psychologists say the infant is so traumatized at birth she instantly develops an unconscious self-defense mechanism that leaves her unable to trust adults. She is convinced that the only one in the world whom she can rely upon is herself.

Whenever I tried to hold her, she flexed in the opposite direction. Her instinct was always to flee, rather than cling. She would not look me directly in the eye. When she was 16 months, I hired a young, spirited Polish nanny who took every pain to care for the baby as if she were her own. But the baby wouldn't bond with her.

During her toddler years, my daughter adapted to nursery school and later to kindergarten. But her patterns with adult care-takers, particularly women, mimicked what went on at home. She was hyperactive, demanding, even charming, but somehow she couldn't be satiated.

It was exhausting. I was exhausted. I didn't know what to do. My daughter was an open, pus-oozing emotional sore I couldn't heal. We were both sinking. I had shut down. On the last day of nursery school during a year-end recital I was shaken from my stupor: when I watched my little girl disrupt the concert, and the nursery school teacher take her aside and restrain her, I cried hard for the first time.

Failing as a mother was unacceptable. That evening I went online and researched Reactive Attachment Disorder, the syndrome that prevents adoptees from attaching. I saw parallels with my child's behavior and suggestions about how to bond and raise these children. Many of the parenting skills needed in these cases are counter-intuitive. That's because a child afflicted by this often doesn't mind punishment or isolation. Unconsciously, that's often the result they're courting.

For the next year, my husband and I focused on trying to interrupt our daughter's hard-wired circuit. We'd say the kind of things you'd never imagine saying to a child such as, "I know you are afraid for mommy to love you. But I do love you." By now I'd realized that punishing her by taking something away had no impact: she was not truly bonded to anyone or anything. She never had a favorite teddy bear or blanket. The best form of punishment was not to punish her at all.

Children afflicted with Reactive Attachment Disorder thrive on chaos and upheaval. It gives them a feeling of control, yet they stay at an emotional distance, which is what they want. Feeling warm and fuzzy causes discomfort. Realizing this, my husband and I undermined our daughter's efforts to cause disruption by responding with calm indifference to fits and taunts. Research on the syndrome says it's important to keep these children off-balance. It disrupts their circuitry, which is a good thing.

Last year when my daughter started first grade, we began to find each other. She still had a hard-wired defense system but now she was exercising an intellect that allowed her to ponder behavior and its effects rather than just act reflexively. She could reach for my hand without feeling deep inner ghosts.

Over time, we knit into a unit. We replaced distance and indifference with fierce love and hate. I don't worry when she tells me she hates me because it shows we're tied up, finally, in the tumult of a mother-daughter relationship.

One day I was walking alone around the lake. Through the brush I spotted a deer milking her fawn. I wasn't more than six feet from them. They saw me too, but the doe kept feeding her young, who couldn't have been more than a few weeks old. I froze in my tracks. Tears streamed down my hot cheeks. I felt a mixture of joy and pain. Here was a gorgeous tableau of primal love. The way nature meant it to be. Something I missed out on. Julia and I were not united by amniotic fluid or mother's milk. We came to each other along an unnatural path, and we stumbled. Slowly we learned to love each other. Because in the end that was the only way it could have happened in our circumstances.

REACHING FOR THE STARS
By Tom Leskiw

High school days, Northern California, 1971. I'd parked my bicycle at a friend's house before leaving with him to party for several hours. Returning stoned, I was in no condition to talk to anyone's parents, but I needed to retrieve my bike. *Quiet as a mouse, now. I'll just slip in and out... nobody will notice a thing.* I was putting the kickstand up, preparing to coast down the driveway, when a voice called to me from the shadows. "Nice night. Just look at the Big Dipper, would you... Simply amazing." Busted. "Yes, Mr. Swindle, it *is* a nice night." Mr. Swindle—Ralph Sr.—was in the mood to talk, so we did. He casually mentioned that his morning had dawned hot and muggy in Singapore. The terms "blow-hard" and "name-dropper" came to mind before I realized that, as an airline pilot for Pan Am, mornings in exotic ports-of-call simply came with the territory.

"Let's move away from the garage, where we can get a better look at the stars," suggested Mr. Swindle. A skilled celestial navigator, he began an impromptu lesson on the glittering constellations high above us in the night sky. "You see the Big Dipper, right?"

"Yes, I do."

"Good. Now follow the curve of the Big Dipper's handle away from the bowl to a bright star, Arcturus. You still with me?"

"Yeah."

"Arcturus lies in the ancient constellation Boötes, which is pronounced 'boo-oh-tees'. This guy Boötes was a herdsman or shepherd. He's found in cave paintings depicting successful hunts of gazelles and zebras in the Sahara. The constellation was named long ago, before the Sahara became a desert."

This was really the first time I'd had an extended opportunity to talk to my pal Terry's dad. Truth be told, I found him an interesting "grup"—Terry's slang at the time for a parent. If Mr. Swindle knew I was high, he never mentioned it. Later, intrigued by our conversation, I pedaled my way home, glancing upward every now and again at the incredible array of stars overhead.

Over the next several years, as Terry and I hung out, I got to know Mr. Swindle better. He and his wife Jewell seemed to be living the good life: a nice home in the leafy green Bay Area suburb of Los Altos, a cabin at Lake Tahoe. They traveled frequently, returning to regale those of us stuck in suburbia with tales of unique cultures, strange customs, and cacophonous marketplaces. Their son and I made an interesting pair, coming from such different socio-economic strata. My parents were divorced and I was the only one of four siblings to live with my father, an emotionally distant, occasionally volcanic-tempered alcoholic. We'd moved to a different high school district so I could attend a school that lacked a dress code. Terry's parents were candid about their reaction to seeing their son bring home "the new boy" — wild hair, part dreadlocks, part white-boy Afro. Over time, however, they saw something in me.

Ralph was a broad-shouldered bear of a man, standing at least 6'4". He never forgot his roots, which he related to me often — much to Jewell's chagrin. "Ralph, stop. The boys don't want to hear about it. *I* don't want to hear about it. Let someone else talk." But there was something about the narrative of his life that grabbed me — one so iconic it could have been a newspaper headline: "Boy from Large Family in Small Town Makes Good." He was born in Priddy, Texas, a small farming community in the central portion of the state, which today has a population of 265. Ralph's size was his ticket out of town, courtesy of a college football scholarship. Later, during World War II, he became a bomber pilot. And when the war was over, he began to fly jets for Pan Am Airlines.

Although I didn't realize it back then, I was constantly on the lookout for surrogate parents — folks who believed in me and weren't afraid to say so. Jewell was a nutritionist and kept working long after Ralph had retired. They were interesting people, as evidenced by the fact that I was but one of Terry's many friends who looked up to them, knowing that we could always come to them for their counsel.

When I was 18, I left the Bay Area for college. I stayed in touch with Ralph and Jewell, and as time passed, I discovered that I had more in common with them than I did their son. When I was 20 years old, an opportunity arose to buy a house and ten acres. I'd saved money from summer jobs and, together with a savings bond from my grandparents, I found myself only $1,000 shy of what the seller wanted for a down payment.

During my high school years, my dad and I had lived in several apartments and duplexes, never staying in one place for long. My pleas for him to buy a place had fallen on deaf ears. Now, two years out of high school, I felt the need to put down some roots. Unlike most of my friends, I had no Plan B: there was no family "homestead" to return to. I had but one chance to borrow the money I needed: Ralph and Jewell. So, I phoned them and said I'd be by that weekend for a visit.

On the way to their house, I rehearsed how to explain my plan to them. "This is my chance to put myself through grad school. I can rent rooms out to students. I'm responsible now. I've calculated I can repay you before two years." I recall the strange mix of doubt, euphoria, and anxiety churning in my stomach as if it were yesterday. *This is my big chance to have my own place. What if they say no?*

Ralph and Jewell loaned me the money, making clear that this was a business proposition: they expected to be repaid within the time frame I'd outlined. The thrill of getting my own place was soon replaced by the reality of being a 20-year-old juggling college, a (nearly) full-time job, and landlord duties. The house needed more work than I'd foreseen, like as a new roof. Long story made short: I did repay them, but missed the deadline I'd outlined. Tough love advocates that they were, the Swindles let me know that I'd disappointed them, but, in time, things returned to normal. I now lived 7 hours from them, so I rarely saw them, except during the holidays. When visiting them, it was a rare day when I didn't encounter at least one of their several "adopted sons."

Where do I start with the life lessons learned from them? Although Ralph never spoke ill of the small town where he grew up, he knew he'd have to leave in order to fulfill his potential. So, "Honor one's roots, yet don't be afraid to reach for the stars" would have to be Lesson #1. Work hard and take advantage of the opportunities that come your way. Over the years, Ralph and Jewell's marriage hit their share of rough patches. I gained insight from watching them on how a successful husband-and-wife team functions. There was always support, of course, but when Ralph needed a "talkin' to," I never saw Jewell shrink from the task. Their travels taught me that the world is a vast, fascinating place where experiencing the unfamiliar lures us outside our comfort zone. The rote is extinguished in favor of fresh perspectives—with personal growth often the result.

From them I learned that Godparents are not only those chosen by your parents at birth, but also include those encountered along the way that mentor, look after you, and lead by example.

Because the Swindles were willing to believe in me, I feel compelled to nurture the continuance of the cycle. I've tried to heed the example they set that a life of fulfillment is best accomplished by reaching outward and helping others. Writing being a passion of mine, I organize, and together with my wife Sue, judge a student nature writing contest. This year, one of the winners came to the awards ceremony accompanied by her grandmother, teacher, and principal. Following the ceremony, I received an e-mail from her teacher, "You can't even imagine how fantastic you made 'Jessica' feel. It was a whole new world for her. Thank you. Thank you." Regardless of the reason for Jessica's parents' absence at the ceremony, it was clear that she was a girl who needed—and was receiving—support from an extended family. And I know from experience just how crucial that can be for someone in need.

WHEN WE LOVE
By Kimberly Alfrey

As I look back on the time spent raising my three children I could easily share many moments that I saw with clarity a moment of truth. Whether that truth was one I truly wanted to see is an entirely different discussion.

As a middle child of a lower middle class family it goes without saying that I had to work and work hard. I was the child least likely to be a parent of the three of us. I often found short cuts in life that I celebrated only to discover that they were the long way around the mountain. My very patient mother did her best to show me the right way, and I did my best to ignore her as I was the wiser teenager. Amazingly my mother has become one of the most intelligent women I know.

Thus, after a failed first marriage I found myself in the proverbial deep side of the ocean without so much as a paddle, raising three amazing children who made me feel much like the ringmaster in a three-ring circus. What you would find some days is that everything went as planned. Then with others, outside forces were ganged up and you were their target. Those days especially were the toughest.

Two people in my life stepped up as my guides. I look back now and clearly see the depth of their love for me and their well intentions have been rewarded by my love as well. I feel there is a special place in heaven for both of these people.

The first was my step-father. An amazing man whom was retired Navy. He was a no-nonsense type fellow who rarely saw the shades of gray. I remember one night when he called and I asked him what he wanted to talk about. He calmly told me that he called to listen, not talk. How incredible. To have someone without a doubt there for you, just to listen while you weather the raising of children alone. Another such night I felt my world was caving in around me; the week, and especially the day, had been horrible.

As I poured out my mess of a day he stopped me, he asked me three profound questions.

"Did I feed my children today" *Of course Dad, duh!*

"Did you kiss them goodnight?" He knew our nightly ritual and thought it was sweet. *Of course, Dad.*

"Do you have a safe place to live?" *Of course.*

His next words I shall never forget. "Then you have had a good day. You need to give a word of thanks to the Lord and celebrate your blessings." Many a night since this night, I have answered these simple questions, then, simply prayed, "Thank you Lord." This took on more meaning when the Lord took Dad to Heaven. I still hear his words of wisdom in my darker days, amazingly simple, but shared with love.

Secondly, I was blessed with an amazing grandmother. Her unique gift was the magical gift of understatement. I remember as I struggled with major decisions in my life. She offered the most profound wisdom in the smallest of ways. Her famous words were, "Think, Kim." Then those would be followed with, "I believe in you." Those simple four words, believe me they meant a lot. She loved me, and she believed in my ability to solve whatever needed to be solved, to accomplish whatever needed to be accomplished.

Beautiful memories now keep me company. As I watch my three angels make their way into adulthood and relish the fact they have made me "Grandma." I often think of the encouragement that I received and I do my best to give what I received. Life is tough, but we all need to know we are loved and that someone just wants to listen. That someone wants to make sure we know how to keep our perspective. That someone believes in us, even when sometimes we don't believe in ourselves. What incredible blessings to give and to share – when we love.

PILLARS HOLD UP A HOUSE
By Leslie Golding Mastroianni

I believe that those who teach music ask more of their students than rote memorization and technical skill. Music draws on the heart and soul. This is the story of Mrs. Virginia Lewis, the choir teacher at my high school, and what she taught a shy young woman about life and architecture.

While growing up in Pittsburg, I found that other than reading, music was my earliest passion and I discovered this at the age of seven, when I began to study the piano. I had, fortunately, an old-fashioned piano teacher who did not wish me to play "easy arrangements" after my first year of study. I began playing the music of Bach, Beethoven, and Mozart when I was eight years old. Because of this, classical music for me would always be linked to nobility, dignity, and virtue. It was as if the spirits of those long dead composers were calling upon me to sit up straight and play my practice pieces three times over instead of the prescribed twice. When I sat at our second-hand upright piano in the dining room and practiced the shorter pieces of these classical composers, I felt uplifted.

When I reached 13, however, I stopped taking piano lessons. Parties, clothes, and boyfriends pulled me away from music and took the place of the great composers. Feminists call this "dumbing down." One of my mother's friends took me aside and warned me against taking this step, but I was afraid of being a "grind." In a magazine for teenage girls, an article appeared titled *Don't Take Yourself Too Seriously*. I didn't want to be too serious, did I? My piano teacher had tears in his eyes when I left, telling me that I was "on the verge of becoming a serious pianist."

Mrs. Lewis came into my life in ninth grade at try-outs for the school choir. The thought of singing in the choir stimulated my dormant love of classical music, and a part of me woke up and didn't care anymore if I was too serious. When I stepped forward to sing for Mrs. Lewis for the first time, I stood in front of her as she sat at her piano, striking notes, telling me to sing and echo what I heard. Her large black eyes looked into mine and I lost all my shyness; all I wanted to do at that moment was sing my very best for this woman who sat up so straight at the piano, shoulders back, commanding, regal.

I began in "C" choir, the lowest, then moved up to "B" choir, where I stayed for 10th and 11th grades. "A" choir, at the top, was reserved for seniors alone; admission to "A" choir was considered an honor. "A" choir performed periodically, for the school and the community.

Mrs. Lewis was Black but nobody recognized this. Nobody called her a Negro, which in 1967 was politically correct. She was a large, tall woman with broad shoulders and dark brown, almost black skin. Her eyes were black and hypnotic, almost magnetic. She could hold you still with her eyes alone. Her posture was magnificent; Mrs. Lewis never slumped over to appear shorter than her true height. She almost always wore sleeveless navy dresses with lighter blue blouses underneath.

Mrs. Lewis was a force of nature. If you thought of defying her, you may as well have tried standing up to one of the great rivers that ran through Pittsburgh. However, none of the choir members feared Mrs. Lewis. We loved her, and we wanted to sing our best for her. By her presence alone she drew our best singing from us. At the beginning of our performances, in the seconds before we drew in our breaths to sing, Mrs. Lewis smiled, big and broad. Her smile was a flashing light, a beacon that said "I'm so proud of you, and you're all going to do great." We seniors of "A" choir felt redeemed by Mrs. Lewis' smile, that all the rehearsals and practicing were worth far more than the effort.

My high school's students were 95% Jewish, but the yearly Christmas concerts were made up of the long, traditional Christmas carols. We sang all the verses of every song from our hearts, including the words "Christ the Savior is born," "Remember Christ our Savior was born on Christmas Day," and "Christ is born in Bethlehem." There was a message here; never verbalized—that music was for everyone. Everybody could rejoice in the festival of lights, and not one Jewish parent complained. *Why? This was Mrs. Lewis.* Even her piano got deluxe treatment; never out of tune, it shone under its coating of lemon-scented furniture polish.

I was happy at the beginning of my senior year. I had a steady boyfriend that was the brass ring on the merry-go-round of teenage life; I was elevated, along with my boyfriend, Sam, into "A" choir that year. One day in October, after choir practice, Mrs. Lewis stood erect as a general at the door of her music room, watching her students file out, always on the alert for gum-chewing and hanging shirt tails, two of her cardinal sins. As I went through the door, she stopped me.

"Leslie, I would like to tell you some good news."

"What is it, Mrs. Lewis?"

"I have selected you to be part of my 'A Capella' group."

"A Capella" was the crème de la crème of achievement in Mrs. Lewis' world; she drew 15 students from "A" choir to sing, without accompaniment, at concerts in school and in the community. Everyone in "A" choir aspired to it, and yearned for admission to it.

I expressed my gratitude and excitement.

"Don't forget; the rehearsals are very heavy and demanding at Christmas time. You know how I feel about my students allowing their schoolwork to suffer."

"Don't worry, Mrs. Lewis, I can do it. I want to do it."

"Good for you. Now I have another piece of news for you. Your boyfriend will not be participating in A Capella."

I flushed and looked down at my feet.

"Do you want to know why? It's because you two are too dependent on each other. You hang on each other. Leslie, picture a building with pillars. What do you see?"

"Uh, well, I'm sorry, Mrs. Lewis. I just see a house."

"That's all right. Tell me then, if somebody tries putting the pillars too close together, what happens to the house?"

"The building and roof are crooked and the building can't stand up and the roof caves in?"

"Yes. You're right. And life is like that. If two people stand too close together and there is no room for light or air, life can't be sustained. Allow some space and light to come between you and others so your house of life won't fall."

I thanked Mrs. Lewis but I thought for the first time that maybe she wasn't as knowledgeable as she appeared. She may have been queen of the music room, but she didn't know the importance of having a steady boyfriend.

Six years passed, two relationships crashed and burned, and the roof on my house of life caved in, just as Mrs. Lewis predicted. But houses can be rebuilt. In this new house, my husband and I stand close enough to see each other and be together; and I think Mrs. Lewis would approve of the fact that there is enough room for light and air to come in, for life to be sustained.

DOGS BARK; THE CARAVAN PASSES
By Erika Hoffman

Almost 89, my dad still has his best buddy, 88. Almost nine decades have passed since his and Tony's childhood in Newark, NJ. Tony grew up down the street from Dad; both attended Weequahic High School; both became the first in their respective families to attend college; both chose engineering as their fields, and both served in World War II in the Pacific theatre. In 1948, Tony stood tall as best man at my parents' wedding. We three kids called him Uncle Tony and didn't realize he wasn't our blood relation until we ourselves were grown.

The Santa doll Uncle Tony gave me as a toddler I kept. I still recall at four sailing with him in Barnegat Bay when my cap blew off. Without complaint, he circled back for it.

Uncle Tony did not marry till age 40. The girl, like him, was of Irish Catholic descent but Canadian and many years his junior, Irene.

As the years passed, our families remained close. Every holiday we shared. In the summer, they with their brood of four gathered round the pool while Dad grilled bratwurst and Irene and Mom fixed the salads and accompanying dishes. Uncle Tony held court.

Uncle Tony asked Dad to be godparent for one of their kids; Tony's youngest child was my flower girl; Irene and Tony picked me up at the airport when I flew up during Mom's hospitalization, and it was Irene who cared for my infant son so I could attend Mom's funeral without having to leave my baby with a stranger.

Three years ago, I packed up my 85-year-old Dad and moved him to my home in North Carolina. Irene and Tony came to help and say good-bye. Dad left behind much of his furniture with them. "It's the end of an era," whispered Tony from his Rascal scooter.

"Mom cried for a week," Irene's oldest told me later. I knew Dad would miss his best friend and his best friend's girl.

For over two decades Tony has been crippled by MS. Now, in a wheelchair he calls "Irene, Irene" repeatedly. She bathes, dresses, cooks, and cares for her husband day in and day out.

"She's a saint," my dad often says. "It can't be easy for her."

They send Dad cards, call him, and cut out clippings from local newspapers to help him remember, to keep him from forgetting his old home, them.

Dad doesn't travel much anymore. He becomes anxious. His short term memory is shot so he's dependent on someone putting him on the right plane, meeting him at the gate, even reminding him of his suitcase, revolving around the motorized luggage belt.

Irene calls up. "Please let your father come stay with us." I'll protest and tell her it's too much on her. "No. We'll have fun. Let him." And, so I do.

I get my courtesy pass, line up the wheelchair, and wait till the plane is airborne before I return home. Fred, a chauffeur, picks Dad up at the gate in Newark, NJ and drives him to Tony and Irene's house. Often, Dad stays two weeks at a time, twice a year.

Irene throws a party, invites old friends, and serves what Dad likes to eat and imbibe. Then, she'll drive him and her Tony to the old neighborhood so the guys can reminisce and note the changes of time. Irene takes them to the Jersey shore where Dad using a cane walks the boardwalk and Tony in his motorized scooter hums along beside him. She carries the two to the nursing home where Dad's sister recuperates from a fall and broken leg. Irene purchases bouquets of roses for Dad and varied flowers for Tony to carry so both men enter the room with a florist's bounty to greet my Dad's 86-year-old sis.

Midway through the stay, Irene phones me to reassure that all is well, and Dad is taking his meds and having a ball. She recites the strict instructions she's given Fred, the limo driver, about accompanying Dad to the gate and waiting till the plane's departure before he himself leaves. "This is what must be done for a nice gentleman like your father," she states.

When I pick Dad up at the airport, he has a spring in his step. "Did you have a nice time?" I inquire.

"Always, I always enjoy myself at the Dennings. Irene's a saint, you know?"

After I lug his suitcase up to his room, I open it and find all his clothes cleaned and pressed.

"Dad," I say," Irene's no saint."

Dad looks up confused.

"She's an angel!" I declare.

Dad smiles, "You can say that again!"

"An angel on earth," I repeat as I carefully take out Dad's ironed shirts.

When I used to think about angels, I always envisioned beatific cherubic looking faces serenely floating around folks and lightly guiding them by the shoulder. Now when I think of those celestial beings, I think of Irene, but she's not an ethereal vision idly floating around fluttering, she's a doer, a pusher of wheelchairs, a hostess with the mostess, a hospitable travel agent who makes all move smoothly, a nurse, a cook, a companion, a cool glass of water on a hot unbearable day. She's not a talker full of unsolicited advice; she is a frank, to the point, no nonsense, and no gossiping sort of gal. She is the type who gets the job done and never complains. Rock-solid, not vaporous, there's not a reality show aired that features folks like her.

My interpretation now of an angel is a person who puts others before herself. Whether it is her genetic disposition, the Canadian environment she was raised in, her deep abiding Catholic faith, or that she was chosen to be blessed by God with the gift of altruism, Irene is an angel who lives in the Garden State and a blessing to anyone fortunate enough to cross her path and call her "friend." She uses her abilities to help those with disabilities. She is the Venus at the altar of Altruism. Dad is a lucky man to merit such friends as Tony and his beloved Irene.

I wrote the above story a couple of weeks ago before Uncle Tony died. Since the funeral, I have been on the phone with Irene a few times. I told her how lucky Tony was to have had her care for him till the end. To which she replied, "I was lucky too."

"Sometimes, Irene, I wish my brother would tell me thanks for taking care of Dad and show me some gratitude, or at least acknowledge that I am doing a good job devoting myself to Dad's care."

Irene listened to me and then she said gently, "Erika, do not wait for someone to praise you or acknowledge your generosity. You know what you've done is right."

"Yes, but…"

"And God knows, Erika. God knows."

So, now when I look for the silver lining to a hideous cloud looming overhead or the good that can come from brutal and unfair criticism, I repeat to myself: "God knows what I am doing. God knows my service."

There is nothing more important than His knowing. If you are doing right and you know it in your heart, then forget the critics, the snipers, and the spiteful. Be like the caravan in the Arab proverb: Ignore the barking dogs and keep moving toward your destination. God's approval is all that matters in the long run, and sooner or later we are all headed toward the same finish line.

ABOUT THE CONTRIBUTORS

Kimberly Alfrey – My essay about my stepfather and grandmother is very special to me. I am thankful for the relationship my patient mother and I now share. I am the mother of three wonderful children, wife to a very special husband and grandmother to two beautiful babies. Life has blessed me in many ways, and I am thankful for family. I have had several poems published, but this is the first of my essays. I'm very proud of this and thankful to have been the "daughter" of Chuck Zagorac and the "granddaughter" of Lois Mixon. May they both be blessed in Heaven.

Diana M. Amadeo – A Multi-award winning author, she sports a bit of pride in having 500 publications with her byline in books, anthologies, magazines, newspapers and online. Yet, she humbly, persistently, tweaks and rewrites her thousand or so rejections with eternal hope that they may yet see the light of day. Her work has appeared in 7 *Chicken Soup for the Soul* books, including *Chicken Soup for the Soul: A Book of Miracles* and *Chicken Soup for the Soul; Celebrating Brothers and Sisters*. She has also appeared in T*he Ultimate Christian Living: Faith and Fellowship and Discover the Awesome Power of the Rosary*. Visit her at http://home.comcast.net/~da.author/.

E. Baker has written on diverse subjects, including *Chinua Achebe: A World Class Writer* (*The New Crisis*). For the New York City Board of Education, she wrote for its ninth-grade curriculum *So You Want a Higher-Paying Job!* She uncovers what is not yet written and shines light there. People living with ills beyond our grasp and show us, without fanfare, what life is truly about move her. Little creative writing covers the immune system and its insidious link to the olfactory (smell) system. Her novel *But for Love* (unpublished) and monograph *Smells Hurt – They Really Do!* are closing the gap.

Lucy Jubilee Barnett is a writer, artist, farmer, and teacher who splits her time between the big city and a small town in Eastern Ontario, Canada. She finds her best ideas while getting her hands dirty in the garden and always needs nature to stroke her soul. Perpetually an observer, Lucy loves to reimage and recreate her experiences through her artwork and writing. The website that details her journey is www.compostellae.com.

Glenda Barrett, a native of Hiawassee, Georgia is an artist, poet and writer. Her chapbook, *When the Sap Rises*, is on Amazon.com, and her paintings are on Fine Art America. Glenda's work has been published in *Country Woman, Mary Jane's Farm Magazine, Woman's World, Journal of Kentucky Studies, Farm & Ranch Living, Chicken Soup for the Soul,* Whispering Angel Book's *Hope Whispers,* and many more.

Judy Shepps Battle has been writing essays and poems long before she became a psychotherapist and sociology professor at Rutgers University. Widely published both in the USA and abroad during the 60's and 70's, she deferred publishing to concentrate on career and family. Fortunately her muse was tenacious and she continued to write during the next three decades filling a file cabinet with scrawled and typewritten material that are now being organized into books and individual submissions. This essay represents her return to active participation in the writing community. She can't think of a better way to spend her retirement.

Francine L. Billingslea – I am a mother, grandmother, a breast cancer survivor and a newlywed for the second time around. I released my inspirational memoir, *Through It All,* in 2009. My recently found passion for writing has led me to be published in several anthologies, including *Chicken Soup For the Soul: Divorce and Recovery, Memories of Mother, Motherwise II, Liberated Muse, How I Freed My Soul Book I, The Rambler Magazine,* online for *Guideposts,* and a contributor to *Hope Whispers,* also published by Whispering Angel Books. I love writing, traveling, and spending quality time with my loved ones.

Justin Blackburn is an Intuitive Inner Healer and the author of four books, including his latest *Female Human Whispers Of Strong Masculine Gentleness* available at www.shadowarcherpress.com. Check him out at www.justinblackburnlovesyou.com.

Kellye Blankenship – I am a mother, daughter, teacher, principal, wife, Christian, & writer. After working many years dedicating my life to public education, I decided to follow a new dream. My hopes are to increase my quality as a Christian, mother and wife and spend a little time sharing my new passion. With God's blessings I will complete my first book by the end of the year. The book tells the true story of a little girl that grows up with an abusive father, allowing the reader an open door to the details. Please contact me at kellyeblankenship@ymail.com or visit my website at http://web.mac.com/kellyeblankenship.

Sharon Bourke is a painter/printmaker as well as a poet. Her poems have appeared over many years in magazines and anthologies such as

Poetry Magazine (Chicago), *Understanding the New Black Poetry* (Wm. Morrow), *Celebrations* (Follett), *Children of Promise* (Harry Abrams), *Songs of Seasoned Women* (Quadrasoul), *LI Sounds 2008* and *2009* (NSPS Press), *Temba Tupu! Africana Women's Poetic Self-Portrait* (Africa World Press), plus non-fiction in the annual journal *Collages & Bricolages*. Her artwork has been used for the covers of two poetry collections, and she is a member of the Graphic Eye Gallery artists' co-op, Long Island, NY.

Ann Reisfeld Boutté has a Master's Degree in Journalism from American University and has been a feature writer for a daily newspaper and a national wire service. A freelance writer, her essays, features and poetry have appeared in many magazines, newspapers and anthologies. She was a Juried Poet in the Houston Poetry Fest in 2001, 2005 and 2009.

A. Frank Bower – Since retiring in April 2006 from mental health work I've published 10 short stories in *Down in the Dirt, Mature Years, Lady Jane's Miscellany, Bewildering Stories, Sangam* and *Glossolalia*. A memoir won 3rd place in the 2009 John W. Paton Storytelling contest at Middletown, CT's Russell Library and a poem took 2nd place in the Altrusa International-sponsored Gerard F. Melito Senior Poetry Contest in central CT this past April. The fall issue of the *Chiron Review* will include one of my poems.

Robin Brown is currently enrolled at the University of Texas San Antonio, where she is actively pursuing her BA in English. She has been a guest reader in a creative writing class at the Alamo Community College District, as well as at Gemini Ink for the Celebrate San Antonio Festival. Her previous publications include the *Coe Review, Slab Literary Magazine, Dreamcatcher Anthology, Origami Condore* and the *Austin International Poetry Festival Anthology*. Robin is working on her first full-length manuscript of poetry entitled *Death of the Break-Up Fish*, which should be finalized and ready to publish by early Fall 2010.

Dr. Milton Burnett, who is licensed in clinical social work, finds his inspiration to write is derived from his varied life experiences, especially those in New York City. He has been published by the Educational Resource Information Center (ERIC) for his medical expertise in assessing and evaluating criteria for emotionally disturbed children and adolescents with substance abuse problems. He can be found on Facebook at Milton Burnett, New Hampshire or reached via email at novadoc@comcast.net.

Helen R. Carson – Ms. Carson started writing poetry in 2007 at the encouragement of a friend who is a many times published poet herself.

Since then her work has been seen in the literary journals *Tapestries, Third Wednesday, Mosaic, Main Channel Voices,* and *Voices of Breast Cancer,* an anthology available at Amazon. Ms. Carson lives with her husband and their cocker spaniel, Sammy, in Southern California where she is a consultant to Native American Head Start programs. When not working she enjoys writing, reading, jewelry design, art photography, needlework, flower gardening, travel, and time with family and friends, especially her six grandchildren.

Elynne Chaplik-Aleskow, Founding General Manager of WYCC-TV/PBS and Distinguished Professor Emeritus of Wright College in Chicago, is an author, public speaker, adult storyteller and award-winning educator and broadcaster. Her non-fiction stories and essays have been published in numerous anthologies and magazines including *Chicken Soup for the Soul, Thin Threads, This I Believe, Forever Friends, The Ultimate Teacher, The Wisdom of Old Souls, Contemporary American Women, My Dad Is My Hero, Press Pause Moments: Essays About Life Transitions By Women Writers* and the international *Jerusalem Post Magazine*. Elynne's husband, Richard, is her muse. To learn more, please visit http://LookAroundMe.blogspot.com.

Elayne Clift is an award-winning writer, a journalist and an adjunct professor in the Humanities at several New England colleges. A senior correspondent for the India-based news syndicate Women's Feature Service and a regular columnist for the *Keene (NH) Sentinel* and the *Brattleboro Commons*, her latest book is *ACHAN: A Year of Teaching in Thailand* (Bangkok Books, 2007). She has just completed her first novel, *Hester's Daughters*, a contemporary, feminist re-telling of *The Scarlet Letter* and is at work on a book about doula-supported birth. She lives in Saxtons River, Vt. www.elayneclift.com.

Jan Cline is a freelance writer, singer, speaker and aspiring author from Spokane, Washington. She has had numerous articles and short stories published and she is currently working on two historical novels. She was recently awarded honorable mention from the Writers-Editors Network International Writing Competition. She has a passion for writing, and loves speaking to encourage and teach women of all ages. You may learn more about Jan at her website: http://jancline.net/ or at her blog: http://janclinewriter.blogspot.com.

Lottie Corley was born Lottie Bishop on October 19, 1963 in San Diego CA. She was raised in Florida, but now lives in North Carolina where she met and married her soul mate Michael Scott Corley. She has finished three of her memoirs: *Truth is Stranger, Trials and Turbulence* and

When Panic Attacks. In addition to writing songs, poetry and articles, she has a huge heart for animals and spends a lot of time rescuing them. Lottie is currently retired and spends most of her time writing and drawing. She is currently working on a book of poems.

Rebekah Crain – I have been writing since I learned how to write. I am always working on stories, essays, occasionally poems, and currently a novel. Nature and people inspire me; I believe each person has a unique and fascinating story. After graduating with a BA in English, I went into the military on active duty. I thought the exposure to new places and people would lead to better, richer stories. Now I work for the Department of the Interior. I am a mother of a fiercely independent, almost big, girl and wife to a resourceful, supportive man.

Ysabel de la Rosa is a writer, designer, and fourth-generation Texan. Her feature writing, poetry and essays have been published internationally in approximately 60 different print and electronic publications. In her "day job," she works as a bilingual editor and publishing consultant to a variety of clients. Her sister Susan, for whom she wrote the essay that appears in this anthology, died on June 23, 2010. Ysabel and Susan's husband were at her side as Susan journeyed from this life to the next. ysabeldelarosa.com, artislingua.com, and ysabeldelarosa.blogspot.com.

Jeanine L. DeHoney is a former early childhood assistant teacher, art enrichment teacher and Family Services Coordinator. She is a freelance writer and has been published in *Chicken Soup For The African American Woman's Soul, Essence, Upscale, Mommy Too, Radiance, Mused Bella-Online, Empowerment 4 Women, Quality Woman's Fiction, Skipping Stones, Bahiyah Woman, Mothering.com, The Write Place At The Write Time, Writing for Dollars, Breathe Again Magazine, 50 to 1, Wow'd Magazine, Literary Mama,* and in *Listen Up Magazine.* Jeanine is married to her childhood sweetheart, and they have three adult children, two daughter-in-laws and a son-in-law and are the proud grandparents of three precious grandchildren that Jeanine loves to dote on.

Bridges DelPonte has written and published two books and numerous articles in the legal and travel fields, including articles for *The Boston Globe, Hemispheres, Richmond Times-Dispatch, The Roanoke Times, Alternatives,* and *LegalZoom.* A Florida Writers Association member, she has completed a mystery novel set in Boston and is currently working on an underwater fantasy novel. Her short story, *Claire de Lune,* will appear in a 2010 Dragon Moon Press anthology. She is pleased to honor her father's memory with this essay. You may e-mail her at bridgesdelponte@yahoo.com and learn more about her writing at her web site, http://www.bridgesdelponte.com.

Laurie Lee Didesch – My work has appeared or is forthcoming in *Aries: A Journal of Creative Expression, The Comstock Review, The MacGuffin, Karamu, White Pelican Review, Rambunctious Review, California Quarterly, ArtWord Quarterly, Artisan: A Journal of Craft, The Awakenings Review, Arts Alive! Literary Review, Northeast Corridor, Jewish Women's Literary Annual, Feast of Fools: Poems, Stories, and Essays on Sacred Fools and Tricksters*, and more. I have also won several awards, including First Place in the Sinipee Writers' Annual Poetry Contest. Most recently, I attended a juried workshop given by Marge Piercy in her hometown on Cape Cod.

Liz Rose Dolan, a five time Pushcart nominee, has won a 2009 fellowship as an established professional from the Delaware Division of the Arts. In addition, her first poetry manuscript was nominated for the Robert Mc Govern Prize, Ashland University. Her second collection, *They Abide*, has recently been published by March Street Press.

Terri Elders, LCSW, lives in the country near Colville, WA, with two dogs and three cats. Her stories have appeared in over three dozen anthologies, including multiple editions of the *Chicken Soup for the Soul, A Cup of Comfort*, and *Patchwork Path* series. She serves as a public member of the Washington State Medical Commission. In 2006 she received the UCLA Alumni Association Community Service Award for her work with Peace Corps. She blogs at http://atouchoftarragon.blogspot.com/. Write her at: telders@hotmail.com or befriend her on Facebook.

Karen R. Elvin has published in art therapy research, journal articles, church newsletters, and currently will soon release a book for children about "Visiting a family member via Alzheimer's." Karen enjoys monthly visits to a health villa where she teaches art & relaxation techniques to residents. For her personal hobbies, she enjoys all art media and creative art quilting. Karen also recently began a new "retirement" ministry and offers Christian Professional Counseling in her Stark County, Ohio community for families who face care-giving responsibilities. She can be reached via email at kelvin@sssnet.com or write to her at 1826 Lake Creek Cir NW, Massillon, OH 44647.

Meredith Escudier, a native Californian, came to France for a year's stint as a student and then watched with some surprise as most of her life unfolded on French soil. Her essays, poetry and memoir have appeared in various anthologies, literary journals and *the International Herald Tribune*. Some of her work can be viewed at www.culinate.com/articles/first_person/the_fig_lover and at www.blablablah.org where she contributes a lighthearted monthly column on language. She enjoys writing about the endearing, the grand and the ordinary, much of which can be found in everyday life.

Robert Fertig is a former adjunct professor Golden Gate University in San Francisco and a 20-year management consultant who has had hundreds articles/stories published nationally and internationally and three business manuals. He is a former central board member of the California Writer's Club and the Bay Area Travel Writer's Club and a former Sunday columnist for the Albany NY Times Union (Hearst). He has three books published, two on travel and another on prostate cancer. His latest book, *How to Travel Like a Pro* will be published soon.

Kathleen Gerard's writing has been widely published and broadcast on National Public Radio (NPR). Her short fiction was awarded the *Perillo Prize*, the *Eric Hoffer Prose Award* and was nominated for *Best New American Voices*, all national prizes in literature. "When Silence Speaks" is an excerpt from *Still Life*, a spiritual memoir. To learn more, visit Kathleen's blog at www.kathleengerard.blogspot.com.

Louise Borad Gerber has written about her life with her 'special daughter', Naomi, both in a memoir, and as poetry. Whereas the memoir is the story of their intertwined lives, the poetry synthesizes the emotional impact, the truths, her realizations, and her ultimate acceptance. Louise has had her poetry published in both Santa Barbara newspapers, and three of her poems will appear in another anthology coming out in September. Her poetry has also won 1st place at the Santa Barbara Writer's Conference. Louise's many careers include: elementary school teacher, mother, special needs activist, artist and business owner. Email: LouiseSBG@gmail.com.

Constance Gilbert retired after 45 years of nursing to Central Oregon. Her passions are to be the "bestest Gramma" and to encourage others through her written words. She is the editor of www.4Him2U.com. She also writes "Connie's Coda" which can be found at http://www.positivelyfeminine.org/Beautiful/beautiful.htm. Her short stories have been published in various anthologies. She currently is stimulating her "little gray cells" by learning Hebrew and writing her first book, *A Forgetful People*. Constance can be contacted via constancegilbert@gmail.com.

Michael S. Glaser is a Professor Emeritus at St. Mary's College of Maryland. He is a recipient of the Homer Dodge Endowed Award for

Excellence in Teaching, and the Columbia Merit Award for his service to poetry in the greater Washington, D.C. area. Widely sought as a speaker and workshop leader, Glaser has served as a Maryland State Arts Council poet-in-the-schools and is active with the Maryland Humanities Council's Speaker's Bureau. He has published over 500 individual poems and eight collections of his poetry. Glaser served as Poet Laureate of Maryland from August, 2004 through August 2009. More at http://www.smcm.edu/poet/.

Evelyn (Eve) Hall is an award-winning author & poet currently living in Georgia. She has authored three poetry and three children's books. Her work has been featured in several magazines and anthologies. Eve has appeared on television and was a featured guest several times on: www.artistfirst.com & www.kruufm.com. She has done several book readings & signings at libraries, bookstores, and schools in Ohio & Atlanta. She just signed an E-book contract for two of her children's books with the publisher at: www.fairytalesanddreams.com. Write her at: cagedbird4u@yahoo.com or connect with her at her blog at: http://mypoeticparadise.blogspot.com.

Erika Hoffman is the author of 70 published articles and non-fiction narratives which have appeared in nationally known anthologies and magazines. She has also written one novel under a nom de plume. Its title is: *Secrets, Lies, and Grace* and it's available through Comfort Publishing.

Cynthia Hollamon-Cook – Cyndee worked as a staff writer for The Advocate at Mount Hood Community College while pursuing a degree in Journalism. She enjoys writing children's stories, poetry, and essays and is currently working on her first novel. In addition to a lifelong interest in writing, she is also an artist. Cyndee is 43 years old and lives in Oregon with her family. Her contact information is: hollamonc@hotmail.com or 1706 Avalon Way #1 Hood River, OR. 97031

Paul Hostovsky's poems have won a Pushcart Prize, the Muriel Craft Bailey Award from *The Comstock Review*, and chapbook contests from Grayson Books, Riverstone Press, Frank Cat Press, and Split Oak Press. He has been featured on *Poetry Daily*, *Verse Daily*, *The Writer's Almanac*, and *Best of the Net 2008* and *2009*. His latest book of poems is *Dear Truth* (2010, Main Street Rag). To read more of his poetry, visit his website: www.paulhostovsky.com.

Floyd E. (Skip) Hughes is an Iowa native and U.S. Air Force veteran. He has lived in many places, most notably for 25 years in Colorado. His daughter, son-in-law, and grandchildren live in Indiana. Through a high school reunion, Skip encountered his sweetheart after over forty years apart. He and Lynne are now happily married residents of Mount Pleasant, Texas. He attended graduate school at a major state university in every state beginning with the letter "O," an academic distinction he thinks might be unique. He currently teaches at Northeast Texas Community College. His published work includes poetry, periodical articles, book reviews, columns, editorial work and photography. His poems have appeared in several anthologies and periodicals.

G. Bennett (Ben) Humphrey – Despite being dyslexic, Ben earned a MD and PhD from the University of Chicago, published papers on his research in Pediatric Oncology, was a reviewer and editor. A retired Professor, he now lives in the Sangre de Cristo Mountains at 9,300 feet. Since he began publishing his poems in 2005, they have appeared in British and American journals, online journals and several anthologies. He frequently participates in poetry readings and conducts workshops. An active member of Poetry West, he has served on its Board of Directors. He can be contacted at 377 Soubry, Fort Garland, CO 81133.

Carolyn Ingram's poetry has been published in *California Quarterly* and *White Pelican Review* and will appear in the *Marin Poetry Anthology, 2010*. Her short fiction has been published in the on-line magazine, *Bust Out*. Recent acknowledgments include Honorable Mention in a poetry contest (*Burning Bush Publications*). She is the co-author of non-fiction books *Have You Ever Been a Child* (Trineheart Publishers, 1995) and *The Not-So-Scary-Breast Cancer Book: Two Sisters Guide from Discovery to Recovery* (Impact Publisher, 2000). A psychologist and coach, she lives with her family in Marin County, California. Visit her at: carolyningram.com. Contact her at carolyn@carolyningram.com.

Marsha Pearl Jamil grew up in rural upstate New York. After graduating from the University of Vermont, she moved to New York to work in magazine and book publishing. She later earned her Masters degree from NYU's Graduate Institute of Book Publishing. After marrying and having three children, Marsha worked as a freelance editor, technical writer and in television advertising. She eventually became the multi-media director for her husband's company. Marsha currently volunteers with a group that selects and donates gently used books to needy libraries and organizations, here and abroad.

Carolyn T. Johnson, a former banker and now freelance writer from Houston, Texas, draws on her colorful life experiences in the US, Europe and South Africa for her poetry, essays and fiction. Her subject matter comes from the heart, the hurt, the heavenly and sometimes the hilarious. She has been published in the *Houston Chronicle* and *Austin American-Statesman* newspapers, *Hope Whispers* anthology, *The Shine Journal, The Calamity Jane* and *Zygote In My Coffee* e-zines and *Tower Notes* newsletter. She also has received a preliminary acceptance from June Cotner's upcoming *Earth Blessings* anthology.

Dale S. Johnson is the author of *The Perfect Wife*, which appeared in the NAACP Image Award-winning Tavis Smiley book, *Keeping the Faith*. Dale has been published in newspapers, magazines and web sites. Most recently his interviews with candidate Obama and Senator Russ Feingold were published in a regional magazine. His current publications are, *Love Passages*, love stories and poems from one man's prospective and *What Every Father Should Know About His Daughter by the Time She is 17...Hopefully*. It explores the unique father/daughter relationship from a very engaging prospective. You can visit him online at www.wordscapesprod.com and contact him at Dale@wordscapesprod.com.

Lynn C. Johnston is the author of *Angel's Dance: A Collection of Uplifting and Inspirational Poetry* and founder of Whispering Angel Books. Her poems and essays have been published in several anthologies, including *Forever Friends, Timeless Mysteries, Antiquities, The World Awaits, Turning Corners, Bridges* and *Hope Whispers*, for which she was also editor. Originally from New York, Lynn is a graduate of SUNY New Paltz. She moved to the Los Angeles area in 1988 where she currently lives with her teenage son. For more information, please visit www.whisperingangelbooks.com.

Charlotte Jones -- After a twenty-year career as a computer scientist and management consultant, she promised herself she would do something more creative with her life and began writing. Her short stories, poetry and essays have appeared in over seventy literary and commercial magazines. She is currently at work on a crime novel for teens and serves on the board of the Women's Institute of Houston, a not-for-profit continuing education organization offering courses in liberal arts. Though her sister died over thirteen years ago, Charlotte still wears a piece of her jewelry every day.

Lucille Joyner pursued a jazz career in New York City until she married and started a family. Her writing was launched when a mayor asked her to ghostwrite and the local editor offered a column. Her stories are published in the Piano Technicians Guild Journal and in a Volvo dealer's newsletter. She is currently working on several books. While she began as a Musician who enjoyed writing, she is now a Writer who enjoys music.

Judy Kirk was born and raised in Plainfield, New Jersey. After thirty some years in advertising, she traded jingles and radio copy for poetry. She spends her days writing poetry, volunteering in schools, and teaches memoir writing for The Guthrie Theater in Minneapolis, Minnesota. In 2007, she published her first chapbook, *Eclipsing the Gray*, a collection of poems about aging. *Straight Through the Heart*, published in March of 2010, is her second chapbook. Her poetry has also appeared in *Hope Whispers*. Judy is a graduate of Indiana University, and lives in St. Louis Park, MN. You may reach her at lilymaepress@earthlink.net.

Rosalie Ferrer Kramer is a published author, poet, and freelance writer. Her book, *Dancing in The Dark: Things My Mother Never Told Me* was published in 1995 and received many glowing reviews. Her poetry and articles have appeared in the San Diego Union Tribune as well as in many local papers. She has written regular column for the Rancho Bernardo Sun and has made several television appearances regarding her book. Rosalie was the mother of two sons who died from Muscular Dystrophy and is now working on a book titled, *Saying and Doing it Right: With the Disabled, the Bereaved and the Fatally Ill*. For more information, go to www.authorsden.com/rosaliefkramer.

Florence Reiss Kraut's short stories have appeared in national confession magazines and magazines for children and her op-ed essays have appeared in Westchester news magazines. Her stories have recently appeared in *The Westchester Review, 2008* and *2009, Rambler Magazine, WriterAdvice, Boston Literary Magazine, Peeks and Valleys, a Southern Journal* and *Pindeldyboz*. She is a social worker and former Executive Director of a family service agency in Connecticut. Currently she lives and writes in Rye, New York and travels widely around the world, which gives inspiration to her writing.

Madeleine Kuderick is passionate about engaging reluctant readers and the teachers who touch their lives. Her work appears in Chicken Soup, Cup of Comfort and several other anthologies. Her story "Cross Roads" was the First Place Winner in the 2010 Thin Threads Best Story competition. In addition to her writing, Madeleine's speaking engagements include conferences hosted by the International Reading Association and the Council for Learning Disabilities. She is a member of the Society of Children's Book Writers and Illustrators, and a graduate of the Institute of Children's Literature. She holds a Master's degree from Saint Leo University. Website: www.madeleinekuderick.com.

Mary Elizabeth Laufer is a freelance writer living in Forest Grove, Oregon. Her poems have been published in magazines, newspapers and several anthologies, including *Proposing on the Brooklyn Bridge* (Grayson Books, 2003), *Hunger Enough, Living Spiritually in a Consumer Society* (Pudding House Publications, 2004), *Hello, Goodbye* (July Literary Press, 2004), *The Dire Elegies, 59 Poets on Endangered Species* (Foothills Publishing, 2006), *Bombshells, War Stories and Poems by Women on the Homefront* (OmniArts, LLC, 2007), and *Beautiful Women – Like You and Me* (BW Books, 2007). "Role Model" was written for her older sister, the poet Nita Penfold, who still inspires her.

Tom Leskiw lives outside Eureka, California with his wife Sue and dog Gypsy. His essays have appeared in a variety of journals, including *Birding; CrossRoads: A Southern Culture Annual; LBJ: Avian Life, Avian Arts; Nature in Legend and Story; Pilgrimage; Watershed;* forthcoming in *Snowy Egret, The Motherhood Muse* (1st place contest winner); and in on-line publications that include Lantern Books (2006 Contest Runner-up) and Terrain.org. Tom retired from the U.S. Forest Service in 2009. He's an avid birder, member of The Association for the Study of Literature and the Environment (ASLE) His monthly column (established 1993) appears at www.RRAS.org and his website resides at www.tomleskiw.com.

Susan (O'Donnell) Mahan -- Born in South Boston, she has been an editor for the South Boston Literary Gazette since 2002. She began writing poetry after her husband died in 1997. She has published four chapbooks, *Paris Awaits, In The Wilderness of Grief, Missing Mum, and World View.* In addition, she has been published in numerous publications and anthologies. "He Called Me Princess" is one of her favorite poems because it reminds her of her husband, whom she misses dearly.

Leslie Golding Mastroianni has a Bachelor of Arts in English Literature from the University of Pittsburgh and a Master's in Counseling from West Chester University. She has been writing for ten years and conducts seminars at Bloomsburg University and other locations in Pennsylvania. She is presently working as a counselor while teaching and facilitating writing workshops. She has been interviewed on local radio about her writing and workshops, which include "I've Always Wanted to Write/Opening the Writer's Eye" and a D.H. Lawrence Seminar. Leslie lives on a farm with her husband and a small herd of pets. She is presently working on a compendium of the lives of working women.

Naty Matos started writing at the age of 14. She was the editor of the school newspaper in both high school and college and also won first place in a school poetry contest. After college, life took over and had to place her writings on hold, but all the while she knew something was missing. In November as part of Nanowrimo wrote her first novel, *The Road Home* that is currently being edited for future publishing. As of December 2009, Naty has been expressing her muses through the blogs therisingmuse.com and trmenespanol.wordpress.com.

Barbara Mayer is a Benedictine Sister of Mount St. Scholastica, Atchison, KS. She is a freelance writer, editor, and poet. She has had poems and stories published in a number of magazines and newspapers, including *The Kansas City Star, National Catholic Reporter, Celebration, Chicken Soup for the Soul,* and *Vocations and Prayer*. She was also a contributor to *Hope Whispers*. Her inspiration comes from Scripture, nature, people, and life experiences. She is in the process of publishing her first chapbook *Behold the Glory*.

Lisa Miles was born and raised in the South Bronx in New York City where she first learned that writing poetry frees the soul. Her poetry has been published by Blue Mountain Arts Inc. She is married with three wonderful children and works as the Affirmative Action Officer for a large university in New York. As an AAO, she has the opportunity to advocate for the differently abled, and was blessed to meet someone who changed her view of the world. Lisa's poem Bend is that story. Lisa recently started a company called Simply Grace, Inc., featuring her poetry as postcards and frameable art.

Beckie A. Miller has published numerous articles and appeared in *Forever Young, Unsent Letter, Writing as a Way to Resolve and Renew* and *Dear Mom, I Always Wanted You to Know*. She is wife, mother and grandmother. She began writing after the murder of her 18-year-old son as an attempt to vent the horrific emotional aftermath of his murder. She has been Chapter Leader of Parents of Murdered Children (POMC) in Phoenix for more than 17 years, and has served on many crime victims' boards and organizations. She has also won numerous awards for her service to crime victims.

Robert B. (Bob) Moreland has a doctorate in biochemistry and works in biomedical/clinical research. He has published poems in the *Bible Advocate,* the *South Dakota Review, Towards the Light, Rope and Wire* and the anthology *Hope Whispers* (Whispering Angel Books, 2009). He has coauthored a book of poems about facing death with Karen M. Miner entitled *Eternal not Immortal* (Trafford Publishing, 2005) and a second collaborative poetry collection with Karen entitled *Postcards from Baghdad: Honoring America's Heroes* (Xlibris Publishing, 2008). Bob resides on the Chiwaukee Prairie in Carol Beach near Lake Michigan in Pleasant Prairie, Wisconsin.

Elaine Morgan is a poet and freelance writer. Her works have most recently appeared in *The Poet's Domain, Wising Up Press, Out of Line, Earth's Daughters, Sacred Journey, Candor, National Assn. of Poetry Therapy*, among many others. She received awards from *ByLine Magazine* and *The Poetry Society of Virginia*. She is a three-time Senior Poet Laureate for the State of Virginia through the Kitchener Foundation. She recently recorded a CD entitled, "*Raining Cats and Dogs,*" a journey of memoir and poetry for those who love and lose their beloved pets. She can be contacted at raining530@yahoo.com.

Eric G. Müller teaches literature and drama at the Hawthorne Valley High School in upstate New York. His first novel, *Rites of Rock* (Adonis Press, 2005), examines the phenomenon of rock music. *Coffee on the Piano for You* is a collection of poetry written mostly while traveling or drinking coffee (Adonis, 2008). His second novel, *Meet Me at the Met* (Plain View Press, 2010) is an in-depth account of a man who endeavors to come to terms with himself and the world at New York's Metropolitan Museum of Art. Articles, short stories, and poetry have appeared in various journals and magazines. www.ericgmuller.com.

Jessica Katsonga Phiri is an author who is inspired by everyday people who live extraordinary lives. She writes with a passion for empowering people to reach their full potential. She publishes a daily devotional at http://bigbeautifulsoul.wordpress.com. Jessica currently holds a position in the educational sector, helping potential students to realize their dreams of returning to school.

Lorraine Quirke is a retiree and new writer with a desire to bring Christians into a deeper faith. She completed the Apprentice Course at the Christian Writers Guild and is a member of the ACFW and Faithwriters. She writes talking animal stories for children, articles and Christian fiction. She has one published article: "*The Promise*" in *Halo Magazine*. *Maxi*, a talking animal story will be published in August in an anthology with Writers Group of the Triad. She resides in Chicago with her cat, Tiffie.

Abi L. Rexrode -- Although born and raised in rural Shenandoah Valley, she now lives in New Jersey. She received a degree in Creative Writing and an award for Literary Achievement from Warren County Community College. The college's literary magazine, *Ars Poetica*, has featured two poems and a short story by her. For Abi writing is more that a hobby; it is as essential to her survival as breathing.

William Ricci is a writer of experimental poems and essays on nature and awareness. Previous work has appeared in: *A View from the Loft, The Edge, Whistling Shade, Paper Darts,* and *Seven Circle Press*. Poetical influences include: D. Nurkse, Nick Flynn, John Haines, and Arthur Rimbaud. He lives on the web at www.provenlife.com

Melanie Rigney is the co-author of *When They Come Home: Ways to Welcome Returning Catholics* (Twenty-third Publications). Her experience includes nearly five years as editor of *Writer's Digest*. To learn more about Melanie, please visit www.melanierigney.com. Melanie lives in Arlington, Virginia.

Joanne Seltzer -- Poems by Joanne Seltzer of Schenectady, New York, have been published in three chapbooks and a variety of journals, including *The Village Voice, The Minnesota Review,* and *Hadassah Magazine*. Her work has been anthologized in *When I Am An Old Woman I Shall Wear Purple, Women Speak to God: The Prayers & Poems of Jewish Women, Hope Whispers,* and many other books. Seltzer's most recent poetry collection, *Women Born During Tornadoes,* was published by Plain View Press in 2009. She is a member of The Authors Guild. For more information about this poet and her work, please visit www.joseltzer.com.

Belinda Sue likes to think of herself as a creative writer/poet who writes about real life. Her first book, *Sahra, the Littlest Angel, Bits and Pieces of Life, Love and Inspirational Messages* (ISBN 1-60441-382-4) contains over 100 poems. Her second book is entitled, *Bits and Pieces of Life* (ISBN 978-1-60976-344-2), and she is currently writing her third book. Her author blog is http://sahra.aegauthorblogs.com/ and work can be found online at www.Scribd.com/mtgirlsal and Facebook.

Janet Tamez is a poet and writer from Union City, New Jersey. She is a survivor of sharing one bathroom with four other siblings. Janet's favorite word is "magenta," and she has never used the word "magpie," ...until now. Many of her poems have been birthed on stage in Miami and New York City. Janet currently teaches creative writing to middle school students in south Florida and earned her B.A. in English from the University of Miami. When Janet is not writing she enjoys spending time with her husband, son, and Mexican hairless dog.

Dana Taylor sold her first magazine article to the *Ladies Home Journal* in 1979. Writing has reflected her life's journey from show scripts for the Sweet Adeline OK City Chorus, published women's fiction novels, to her interest in energy healing and alternative medicine in her upcoming book, *Ever-Flowing Streams: Adventures in Prayer*. She hosted the Internet radio show Definitely Dana! at HealthyLife.net. and won several awards from chapters of the Romance Writers of America. Find her on the web at SupernalFriends.com, Amazon.com, Scribd.com, Smashwords.com, and Facebook. Contact her at supernalfriends@yahoo.com.

Paula Timpson is the author of The Spirit Series Poetry Books, which are currently on Amazon.com. To learn more about Paula, please visit her website blog at: http://paulaspoetryworld.blogspot.com.

Tina Traster writes the Burb Appeal column for the *New York Post* and the Great Divide blog for *The Huffington Post*. Her work has appeared in newspapers, magazines, literary journals, NPR and on online literary web sites. Traster's notable work is archived on her website: tinatraster.com. Traster is at work on a memoir about becoming a suburbanite. She lives with her husband, daughter, four cats and six chickens in an old farm house in Rockland County, NY.

Claudia B. Van Gerven -- I live in Boulder, Colorado, where I teach writing. My poems have been published in a number of journals and magazines including *Prairie Schooner, Calyx,* and *The Lullwater Review*. My work has appeared in numerous anthologies and has been nominated for the Push Cart Prize. My chapbook, *The Ends of Sunbonnet Sue*, won the Angel Fish Press Poetry Prize and my full-length manuscript, *The Spirit String*, has been a finalist in three national contests.

Andrea L. Watson's writing has appeared in *Runes, Ekphrasis, Cream City Review, Subtropics, The Dublin Quarterly, International Poetry Review, Nimrod* and *Memoir (and)*. Her show, *Braided Lives: A Collaboration Between Artists and Poets*, founded with artist Seamus Berkeley, was inaugurated by the Taos Institute of Arts and has traveled to San Francisco, Denver, and Berkeley. She is co-editor of *Collecting Life: Poets on Objects Known and Imagined*, forthcoming from Iris Press.

Neal Whitman -- In 2005, at the start of his phased retirement from the education profession, Neal Whitman took up the poetry profession. He writes both Western form and Japanese haiku. In 2009, he won first prize in the James McIntyre Poetry Contest in Ontario, Canada, and two haiku were awarded honorable mention in the Yuki Teikei Haiku Contest judged by haiku masters in Japan. In 2010, Neal won 3rd prize plus honorable mention in the *Common Ground Review* poetry contest. Neal and his wife, Elaine, are Unitarian Univeralists, and he delivered a version of this essay as a "Call to Worship" at Sunday Service.

Cherise Wyneken is a freelance writer who found joy late in life through writing prose and poetry. Selections of her work have appeared in a variety of publications including *Hope Whispers,* two books of poetry, two poetry chapbooks, a memoir, a novel, and a children's book. She is a member of the Bay Area Poets Coalition, the Women's Potluck and Poetry Salon, and enjoys reading her work at various other local venues. She is the mother of four, grandmother of eight, and lives with her husband in Albany, CA. http://www.authorsden.com/cherisewyneken http://givingbooks2kids.com.

WE WANT TO HEAR FROM YOU

Has one or more of the stories touched your heart? Has it made you think differently about your own situation? We would like to hear your thoughts or comments.

Do you have a short story or poem that you'd like to see in a future Whispering Angel Book? If so, please go to our website for upcoming book topics and submission guidelines.

Whispering Angel Books is dedicated to publishing uplifting and inspirational stories and poetry for its readers while donating a portion of its book sales to charities promoting physical, emotional and spiritual healing. We also offer fundraising programs to help you increase revenue for your charitable organization. If you'd like more information, please contact us.

To contact us or to order additional books, please visit:

www.whisperingangelbooks.com

www.ingramcontent.com/pod-product-compliance
Lightning Source LLC
Chambersburg PA
CBHW031246290426
44109CB00012B/455